Return of Assassin John Wilkes Booth

W.C. Jameson

John Wilkes Booth
(Reproduced from the collections of the Library of Congress)

Return of Assassin John Wilkes Booth

W.C. Jameson

Republic of Texas Press

Library of Congress Cataloging-in-Publication Data

Jameson, W. C., 1942-.
Return of assassin John Wilkes Booth / W.C. Jameson.
p. cm.
Includes bibliographical references and index.
ISBN 1-55622-642-X
1. Booth, John Wilkes, 1838-1865. 2. Assassins—United States —Biography. 3. Fugitives from justice—United States—Biography. 4. Lincoln, Abraham, 1809-1865—Assassination. I. Title.
E457.5.J35 1998
973.7'092—dc21 98-29861
[b] CIP

Republic of Texas Press is an imprint of Wordware Publishing, Inc.

Printed in the United States of America

ISBN 1-55622-642-X
10 9 8 7 6 5 4 3 2 1
9807

All inquiries for volume purchases of this book should be addressed to Wordware Publishing, Inc., at 2320 Los Rios Boulevard, Plano, Texas 75074. Telephone inquiries may be made by calling:

(972) 423-0090

Contents

Preface

Virtually every American knows the name John Wilkes Booth. Surveys have confirmed that for most citizens of the United States, even the world, the infamous actor, along with his most famous deed, is synonymous with the word "assassination."

Mention the name John Wilkes Booth, that noted and magnetic thespian of the mid-nineteenth century, and all but a sheltered few immediately associate it with the murder of President Abraham Lincoln. Even today, according to author David Robertson, Booth, an enigmatic, attractive, manipulative, and violent character, "continues to command the American imagination in a way not fully explained by the facts of his life or his notoriety."

Indeed, to this day, John Wilkes Booth remains a looming, gnawing enigma, among the most complex and puzzling in American history. Rising well above the confusing and tangled web of mysteries embracing the actor are the ones associated with the distinct possibility of his escape and return.

I remember as a child the few occasions when family members brought up the subject of John Wilkes Booth. It was done in hushed tones accompanied by furtive glances at the doors and windows as though the speakers feared someone might be listening. On those rare occasions when I chanced to enter the room during such conversations, the subject was immediately dropped and another quickly substituted. I was too young to understand, or even care, about the family secrecy surrounding this historical character.

When I was ten years old and in the fifth grade, I was subjected to an elementary school lesson in history that included facts on the tenure of Abraham Lincoln as president of the United States and his role, as they said in those days, in "freeing the slaves." We also learned that Lincoln was assassinated in his prime by John Wilkes Booth, an actor, who was eventually captured and killed several days afterward.

So said the textbooks.

On arriving home that afternoon, I excitedly related portions of the day's lesson to family members and some guests who were visiting. When I got to the part about John Wilkes Booth, I was immediately shushed and sent to another room.

Later, after company had departed, I was reprimanded for bringing up the subject of Booth and told never to do it again. When I asked why, the answers stunned me then as they stun me today. First of all, I was told, John Wilkes Booth was kin. To many, my family foremost among them, being related to a political assassin was considered a socially unacceptable position in which to be in those days, so the matter was kept secret. Second, the assassin was rarely spoken of by tacit agreement among surviving relatives because, they believed and I was told, *John Wilkes Booth was never captured and killed by government authorities, but escaped to live for many years afterward.*

The prospect of being related to a notorious assassin generated mixed emotions in a ten-year-old. On the one hand, I was honor-bound to maintain the secret. On the other, the revelation that Booth had escaped generated in me a burning curiosity about the man and his life and times, a curiosity that has not yet abated in the more than four decades since. Beginning at that young age, I read everything I could find about Abraham Lincoln, the Civil War, the politics of that era, and, of course, John Wilkes Booth.

The more I read, studied, researched, analyzed, and considered the traditional histories of these subjects, the more I came to realize and appreciate what I now perceive to be the truth of what I was told as a youngster:

John Wilkes Booth escaped.

Chapter I

Introduction

What is the truth about John Wilkes Booth?

What really happened to what many historians contend is the world's most famous political assassin?

History records that John Wilkes Booth, on the evening of 14 April 1865, assassinated President Abraham Lincoln. Of that there can be little doubt since dozens in attendance at Ford's Theater witnessed the killing and/or the escape of the actor.

History also records that, following a twelve-day pursuit, John Wilkes Booth was finally trapped in a barn on the Virginia farm of Richard Garrett. Shot while resisting capture, the mortally wounded fugitive was dragged from the structure, which had been set on fire, and carried to Garrett's front porch where he died a short time later.

Of this particular event, unlike the assassination of Lincoln, there is overwhelming doubt and confusion. Almost from the moment the dying man was pulled from the burning barn, it was being whispered that he was *not* John Wilkes Booth. As events of the next forty-eight hours unfolded, the complications and confusion concerning the identity of the man did not abate. Instead, they grew and swelled to such proportions that government authorities were put to the task of writing and issuing informational releases on the matter. Rather than quash the rumors of Booth's escape, they only added to the confusion.

Significant doubt and contradiction surfaced during the subsequent inquest, identification, and burial of the body—doubt and contradiction borne of obvious governmental fumbling, ineptitude, and dishonesty. Conspiratorial overtones strongly hint at governmental deception and cover-up regarding the identity of the body being offered as that of the assassin.

Today, most researchers are convinced that all of the facts pertinent to events and participants associated with the conspiracy to assassinate President Lincoln will never be known. Perhaps.

Many are likewise convinced that the truth pertaining to the identity of the man killed at Garrett's farm on 26 April 1865 will never be known. If it was not Booth, then who was it?

What we know, or what we think we know, of the capture and killing of John Wilkes Booth has been derived primarily from historians' interpretations of government documents written well over a century ago. Critical examination of these documents, as well as representations of them by scholars and writers over the years, reveal obvious and, in some cases, somewhat embarrassing elements of confusion and contradiction. Following intensive research into said materials, coupled with logical analysis, along with deductive and inductive reasoning, it is difficult to come away from the experience without a number of serious doubts—doubts about what actually occurred; doubts about the role of several highly placed government officials; doubts relative to the number, identity, and role of the conspirators; doubts concerning the identity of the body that has been passed off as being that of John Wilkes Booth.

Adding to these doubts, as well as filling in some important historical gaps, are the relatively recent discoveries of a number of important documents. Compelling and revealing information in the form of papers and diaries have recently been found in private collections, materials which provide greater insight into the events leading up to the assassination as well as details of the pursuit and capture of the man the government claimed was Booth.

Stunning evidence supporting the notion that Booth escaped is found in the Andrew Potter papers. These documents, compiled by federal policeman Andrew Potter, are part of a collection in the possession of scholar Dr. Ray Neff of Indiana State University and examined by researchers and writers David Balsiger and Charles E. Sellier Jr. Andrew Potter, an officer on Colonel Lafayette Baker's National Detective Police agency, the nation's precursor to the Secret Service, played a major role in the pursuit of John Wilkes Booth in the days following the Lincoln assassination.

If authentic, and there is no reason to doubt otherwise, the Potter papers provide provocative and compelling evidence that John Wilkes Booth was neither captured nor killed, but instead escaped to live for many years.

In addition to the Potter papers, Balsiger and Sellier examined long-lost personal papers of Secretary of War Edwin M. Stanton, as well as a number of other important documents.

This new information, along with a critical reexamination of the traditional historical materials and interpretations, provide more than sufficient reason to challenge the general and long-held assumption that John Wilkes Booth was killed by government agents in Virginia. In truth, a greater body of evidence now exists supporting the notion that Booth effectively escaped pursuit and that a Union spy, a Booth look-alike, actually perished at Garrett's farm.

This book presents the case that John Wilkes Booth, the assassin of President Abraham Lincoln, was never captured. Furthermore, startling evidence is offered that supports the contention he escaped to live a relatively long life, continue his acting career, marry, and have children.

What happened to John Wilkes Booth following his escape? Over the years, a number of men have been identified as being Lincoln's assassin. Some of these men were clearly impostors, others were simply victims of mistaken identity. One or two, however, are hard to dismiss, and the evidence surrounding their identities as Booth has puzzled researchers for years.

In the end, you be the judge.

Chapter II

Who Was John Wilkes Booth?

Beyond his specific identity and notoriety as the man who assassinated President Abraham Lincoln, very few are aware of the complexity and depth of the curious and tragic historic figure John Wilkes Booth.

Even fewer are aware of the confusing and bizarre sequence of events and consequences related to the pursuit and killing of the man believed to be Booth—events and consequences that remain a mystery to this day.

John Wilkes Booth was one of the most successful actors of his time, and it has been written that he was the finest actor ever to grace the American stage. In spite of his theatrical successes, many have dismissed him as a mere lunatic. Some historical accounts have referred to him as a crazed actor. A number of researchers and writers have labeled him a "Satanic genius," "a mad zealot," "a villain from the cradle," "a half-demoniac creature of savage instincts," and a "vulgar cut-throat activated by a thirst for notoriety." In *The Great American Myth*, author George S. Bryan referred to Booth as a ham actor, boisterous, lazy, devoid of talent, ranting, coarse-grained, shy, trivial, and vain.

Others have claimed Booth was an emissary for the Roman Catholic Church, an officer in the Knights of the Golden Circle, and a hired accomplice of Vice President Andrew Johnson. There exists, however, no evidence whatsoever that any of these descriptions fit the character that was John Wilkes Booth.

Booth was, among other things, a passionate and patriotic son of the South who gave himself wholeheartedly to the Southern cause with a devotion and fervor unmatched. Booth's niece, Blanche de Bar Booth, was quoted by the actor's biographer Francis Wilson as saying that Booth was "loved for his kindly nature, his generosity, and the qualities of a refined gentleman convinced that he had good reason to slay Lincoln, and he was not alone in his thinking."

John Wilkes Booth was the child of Junius Brutus Booth and Mary Ann Holmes, the fifth of six children of that union who survived to maturity. In all, Junius had ten children. Since Junius and Mary Ann were not married at the time, all of the American-born Booth children were technically bastards.

Junius Brutus Booth was born in London in 1796, and by the time he was seventeen he was performing regularly in theaters throughout England and receiving wide acclaim for his work. The elder Booth arrived in America in 1821 and one year later purchased a farm near Belair, Maryland, some twenty miles from Baltimore.

Junius Brutus Booth soon became one of America's most noted Shakespearean actors, was regarded as the most prominent actor of his day, and performed throughout much of the eastern part of the United States. He remained popular with American audiences for three decades. In addition to being a superb thespian, Junius Brutus was also considered to be a linguist, playwright, scholar, and philosopher. He was also a hopeless and pathetic alcoholic.

John Wilkes Booth was born 10 May 1838 in the small town of Harford, Maryland, some three miles east of the Belair farm. He was the second youngest and was named after John Wilkes, the eighteenth-century British reformer and political agitator who made a strong impression on Junius. Wilkes opposed practically everything about the rule of British King George III and served for a time as the British representative of a Boston-based revolutionary group.

Called Johnnie by his father and siblings, young John Wilkes Booth was brought up by Junius to respect and champion the ideals of liberty and to never tolerate tyranny of any kind.

The elder Booth raised his children in aristocratic luxury on Belair's 150 acres. He constructed a brick, English-style cottage he called Tudor Hall, planted an orchard and vineyard, and supervised the construction of stables, a large swimming pool, and slave quarters. The Booths were never without servants and slaves, and Junius Brutus was always kind and liberal with them.

In this environment, young John received a proper education as well as instruction in riding. He even broke and rode his own horses. John was sent to schools in and near Baltimore but spent summers on the estate. He attended St. Timothy's Hall at Catonsville, an Episcopal academy with a military curriculum where he learned how to shoot rifle and pistol. According to all reports, he became an excellent marksman.

Author George S. Bryan writes that Booth's fellow students remembered him as one who sought notoriety and who often spoke of doing something of sufficient impact that he would always be remembered and recognized. At

St. Timothy's, Booth met Sam Arnold, a fellow student who was to play an important part in his future.

John Wilkes Booth grew up rather spoiled and snobbish and manifested an air of elitism unlike most of his playmates. He was often moody and sullen. Booth seldom concealed his distaste for the family's black slaves, and he never deigned to engage in conversation with the hired help, black or white. Though he listened to and enjoyed the music of the blacks, he held them in contempt as human beings.

Booth also, at times, demonstrated a vicious temper. Once, during a play rehearsal when a promoter was lagging behind schedule, Booth grabbed a piece of wood from a set and flung it hard at the man, barely missing his head and causing serious injury.

Booth deplored immigrants of any kind, particularly Irishmen. He attended meetings of the Know-Nothings and the American Party, two organizations opposed to foreign immigration and the political influence of immigrants and Roman Catholics.

John's brothers were Junius Brutus Jr., Edwin, Joseph, Frederick, and Henry Byron; his sisters were Asia, Rosalie, Mary Ann, and Elizabeth. Junius Brutus Jr. and Edwin were both fine actors but never received any instruction from their famous father. Joseph had a brief fling with the stage but lacked the skills and presence of his famous parents and siblings.

Though he was only thirteen years old when his father died, John learned much about the craft of acting at his father's side. As he gained theatrical prominence in later years, many commented that he had obviously inherited a fine and rare talent from Junius Brutus Sr. Brother Edwin once stated that John could have become one of the most brilliant actors in the world.

John Wilkes Booth
(Library of Congress photo)

John Wilkes Booth made his acting debut in 1856 when he was seventeen years old, a minor role in *Richard III*. It was a disaster—he suffered a severe case of stage fright and forgot his lines. The performance was so bad the audience booed him and the newspapers panned his performance. John, in ill temper, sulked for days and swore he would never act again.

Two summers later, however, he performed as Horatio in *Hamlet* in Richmond, Virginia, to cheers and raves. In 1860 Booth joined a theatrical company that toured throughout the South. His performances were spirited and dynamic, and he soon played to packed houses and rave notices. Women screamed during his curtain calls and often threw roses on the stage at his feet. Booth's career as an actor was on the rise.

As a young man, John Wilkes Booth manifested a passion not only for acting but for politics, often working himself into a lather over the topics of secession, slavery, and President Abraham Lincoln. Booth sided strongly with the South, supported secession, and considered abolitionists to be tyrants. He often spoke of the Confederacy as "his country." So violent and angry were his arguments that brother Edwin forbade political discussions when John came to visit.

Between 1861 and 1864, Booth was in great demand as an actor and toured extensively throughout the North, South, and Canada. He was paid about $20,000 per year, an impressive sum at the time.

During April 1863, Booth played his first engagement in Washington, D.C. at Grover's Theater. The play was *Richard III*. Among the large and fashionable audience that attended the 11 April performance was President Abraham Lincoln.

In addition to his growing celebrity status, Booth was quite handsome and he became a favorite with the ladies. Following a string of successful performances in Washington, women began following him through the streets asking for his autograph. They were drawn to him, as writer Theodore Roscoe states, "like pins drawn to a magnet."

Booth reveled in the attention. He even dressed the part—a fawn waistcoat, a long black coat with velvet lapels, trousers with heel straps, a wide-brimmed hat, an expensive and prominently displayed cameo, and a bamboo walking cane.

Booth is believed to have had many lovers, several mistresses, and, though shrouded in mystery, at least one wife. He was known to consort with a noted prostitute of the day named Ella Turner, also known as Ella Starr, Nellie Starr, and Fannie Harrison. In Manhattan, Booth lived for a time with Sally Andrews and was believed to have promised marriage to a woman named Anne Horton. Some researchers include the widow Mary Surratt among Booth's romantic flings. Surratt was ultimately executed for her role in the conspiracy to assassinate President Lincoln.

Booth also had romantic, and apparently sexual, inclinations toward actresses Fanny Brown, Alice Grey, Effie German, and Helen Western. In fact, pictures of these four, along with a fifth, were found among Booth's possessions. The fifth was Bessie Hale, the daughter of Senator John P. Hale, a noted anti-slavery advocate. Booth and Bessie Hale were engaged to be married even while he was dallying with actresses and prostitutes.

A number of scholars are in agreement that there is a possibility Booth was secretly married to Izola D'Arcy Mills in 1859. Mills, a devoted Southerner, was believed to be active in smuggling quinine and morphine into the South.

Booth also possessed a dark side when it came to women. He was once reported for rape in Philadelphia and was severely beaten in an adultery incident in Syracuse.

For a time, Booth worked clandestinely for the South and its hoped-for success. He once admitted to his sister Asia that he was a secret agent, a spy, and that he entered the Rebel underground during the winter of 1863. When the opportunity arose, he smuggled bandages and medicine, mostly quinine, to the Southern troops and was known to many of them as "Dr. Booth." During this period, Booth himself may have begun using drugs.

In addition to medicine, Booth carried important information to Southern leaders. To what degree he engaged in spying is not completely known, and the truth about Booth's espionage activities is yet to be uncovered.

Booth's passion for the South grew dramatically during the early 1860s. Asia's husband, John Sleeper Clarke, regarded Booth as monomaniacal on the subject and refused to engage in discussions with him. Older brother Junius also expressed concern for John's unbridled enthusiasm for the Southern cause and his vitriol against the Union and President Abraham Lincoln. More and more, it seemed, John Wilkes Booth blamed the country's growing problems on the president—he despised Lincoln and all that he stood for.

John Wilkes Booth was five feet, eight inches tall, slightly above average for the time. Author David Miller Dewitt described his face as "remarkably handsome." Booth's sister Asia wrote that he possessed his father's "finely shaped head and beautiful face." The head was topped with thick, wavy, glossy, jet-black hair, and a moustache decorated his upper lip, one that turned down somewhat at the ends, providing him with a certain roguish air. Though Booth has most often been described as having piercing and penetrating black eyes, sister Asia wrote that he had large, expressive hazel eyes similar to those of his mother, eyes set deep under heavy lids.

Author George Alfred Townsend said of Booth:

> He had one of the finest, vital heads I have ever seen . . . one of the best exponents of vital beauty I have ever met . . . health, shapeliness, power in beautiful poise, and seemingly more powerful in repose than in energy. His hands and feet were sizeable . . . and his legs were stout and muscular. . . . From the waist up he was a perfect man; his chest . . . full and broad, his shoulders gently sloping, . . . his arms . . . hard as marble. [He had] a fine Doric head, spare at the jaws . . . seamed with a nose of Roman model.

Booth's hands were noticeably large and, according to research, he was right-handed. As a child, wrote his sister Asia, he tattooed his initials, "JWB," on the back of one of his hands in India ink. Unfortunately, Asia did not specify which hand bore the tattoo, an omission that was to contribute heavily to a deep mystery in later years.

Booth also possessed a number of scars on his face and body. One of the most prominent was the result of a deep wound on his forehead, the result of being struck as a youth by a thrown oyster shell.

Booth was quite athletic, "well-knit and well-proportioned," according to writer Bryan, and an excellent horseman, swordsman, and gymnast. Dewitt wrote that he was "noted for his extraordinary leaps on stage."

Offstage, Booth was a gentleman, charming, high-minded, cultured, eloquent, gracious, kindly in manner, a good listener, generous with his money and time, and, as Bryan states, "devoid of petty vanity."

That John Wilkes Booth, at twenty-six years of age, killed President Abraham Lincoln is not open to question. He most assuredly did, and it is a matter of certain and unassailable historical fact.

The events following the assassination, however, are another matter entirely. Though the escape, pursuit, and death of the assassin have been extensively researched and written about hundreds of times since 1865, there remains overwhelming doubt relative to what actually happened to John Wilkes Booth.

Chapter III

Plots To Kidnap

During the first week of March 1864, Union brigadier general Judson Kilpatrick led a raid into Richmond, Virginia, for the stated purpose of releasing over one hundred Federal prisoners held there. Kilpatrick assured President Abraham Lincoln during a meeting on 13 February 1864 that the Confederates were expecting nothing and the plan should succeed.

The strategy called for Kilpatrick to approach Richmond from the north with a large cavalry force accompanied by artillery. Colonel Ulric Dahlgren was to lead another contingent of cavalrymen, all dressed in Confederate uniforms, across the James River and attack Richmond from the south. After freeing the prisoners from the Belle Isle prison, he was to rejoin Kilpatrick's troops at about the time Richmond was being attacked.

Following a positive beginning, things began to go terribly wrong for Dahlgren. During the early part of the raid, Dahlgren's soldiers destroyed a number of gristmills and a sawmill and sunk several boats loaded with grain. In addition, canal locks and a coal mining operation were destroyed.

Rather than terrify the Southerners into flight, however, Dahlgren's raid only served to infuriate them. Grabbing weapons, the Southerners took to the woods and began sniping at the Dahlgren force, picking off men at an alarming rate. So great was the resistance that Dahlgren ordered a retreat.

By the time Dahlgren and his command reached the Rapidan River, they found it flooded from recent rains and impossible to cross. As he pondered the best course of action, a scout informed him that Southern marksmen were closing in, inflicting serious casualties.

Dahlgren led his men downstream in search of a ford. Within minutes they rode into an ambush, and Dahlgren, along with twenty of his troopers, was killed. One hundred more were captured.

On Colonel Dahlgren's body were found two sets of papers that many historians claim eventually led to the death of Abraham Lincoln. The first was a letter, written by Dahlgren, stating that after freeing the captives, their intention was to enter Richmond, destroy the bridges behind them, and exhort the released prisoners to "destroy and burn the hateful city; and . . . not allow the rebel leader, Davis, and his treacherous crew to escape."

The second paper was a written, yet unsigned, order that stated once inside Richmond, Dahlgren was to destroy the city and kill Jefferson Davis and his cabinet.

When news of the documents spread throughout the Southern countryside, Confederates were furious.

Lincoln, who had been seeking peace with the South, was puzzled by the documents, for he had made no such orders.

There were two immediate and unfortunate results of the failed Dahlgren raid. For one, peace negotiations that were secretly being conducted in Nashville, Tennessee, were destroyed. For another, the Lincoln administration and leadership were cast into doubt, with members of the president's own party already making plans to abandon him in the upcoming election in favor of Salmon P. Chase.

Contrary to the perceptions of most Americans at the time, President Abraham Lincoln was probably far more hated than he was loved. He was hated not only by Southerners, but by a surprising number of Northerners as well.

According to Lincoln researcher and author William Hanchett, President Lincoln was despised "for attempting

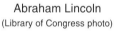

Abraham Lincoln
(Library of Congress photo)

to force the South to remain in the Union, for usurping cherished constitutional rights, for pursuing a policy regarding slavery that would lead to the Africanization of the United States, for degrading the presidency, for shedding so much blood, for making so many widows, and for creating so many fatherless homes."

Lincoln had been marked for assassination on the very day he was elected. Southerners loudly and often boasted of traveling to Washington to slay the president. At various times during Lincoln's tenure as the country's leader, dozens of Confederate soldiers, viewing him as an obstacle to Southern independence, offered to assassinate him. Some Southern citizens even took out ads in local newspapers volunteering to do the deed. Dozens of plots to kidnap or assassinate Lincoln were known of since 1861.

Though some were convinced Lincoln was a great president and leader, those who hated him perceived him as vulgar, unrefined, uneducated, obscene, vicious, brutal in habits, filthy, a boor, a coward, a drunk, and a clod.

As early as the first week of August 1864, Abraham Lincoln was informed by U.S. marshal Ward Lamon about recent rumors of assassination attempts. Lamon, Lincoln's former law partner, was regarded by many as being the president's best friend. According to writer Margarite Spalding Gerry, Lincoln responded to Lamon's concerns by telling him, "Assassination is not an American practice. If anyone was willing to give his own life in the attempt to murder a president, it would be impossible to prevent him."

What Lincoln could not know at the time was that the most serious threat to his life was from a man he knew of but had not met—John Wilkes Booth.

During the early part of 1864, a small group of planters assembled just outside the small, quiet community of

Bryantown, Maryland. Over drinks, they discussed strategies pertinent to ending the war. The meeting was called by one Patrick C. Martin and included two physicians—Dr. William Queen and Dr. Samuel Mudd.

During the meeting, one of the participants suggested the best way to end hostilities was to kidnap the president and turn him over to Jefferson Davis. At first the idea was rejected as being reckless and foolhardy, but as the discussion proceeded, interest in such a plot grew. After a time, most agreed that if Lincoln could somehow be removed from office, the war might quickly come to an end.

Eventually the idea of kidnapping Lincoln took on a life of its own, and the planters began to seriously consider a scheme. The first question raised was related to finding a suitable individual to commit the act. Several names were suggested and all rejected for a variety of reasons.

Martin told the others he knew a man who would be capable of arranging and accomplishing a kidnapping. When the participants asked who, he replied: John Wilkes Booth.

By way of providing credentials, he told those assembled that Booth was a Maryland native, passionately loyal to the South and the Southern cause, had demonstrated his allegiance to the South in a number of ways, and was very eager to become involved.

More discussion followed, and by the time the meeting concluded, all were agreed that Martin should arrange a meeting with Booth to discuss the proposed abduction.

During the war, hundreds of Confederate soldiers who escaped from Union prisons fled across the border into Canada. For the most part, they remained in that foreign country, living among the natives and awaiting the opportunity for hostilities to cease so they could return to their homeland.

In April 1864 Confederate president Jefferson Davis appointed Jacob Thompson and Clement C. Clay as special commissioners to Canada. Thompson was from Mississippi and was once the secretary of interior in the cabinet of former president James Buchanan. Clay, a former Alabama state senator, was currently serving as a senator for the Confederate States of America. The two appointees joined other Confederates already operating in Canada, among them Beverly Tucker of Virginia and George N. Sanders of Kentucky.

In Canada, the Southerners had orders to work for the defeat of Lincoln in the approaching fall election by buying up influential newspapers. They were also to encourage the Rebel soldiers living in Canada to conduct raids against American towns located just across the border.

In June, three months after the failed Dahlgren raid, Colonel William A. Browning, the private secretary to Vice President Andrew Johnson, visited Washington D.C.

During his stay in the capital, Browning ran into an old acquaintance, the actor John Wilkes Booth. Booth asked Browning about the raid and was told that the Confederates faked the papers found on Dahlgren in an attempt to bring embarrassment to the Union.

Booth then surprised Browning with a comment about the ongoing and secret peace negotiations. Shocked, the secretary asked the actor how he knew of such things and Booth merely replied that he had many friends in the South. With such connections, Browning suggested to Booth that he might be able to find a role for him in helping to reestablish the peace discussions. Booth replied he wasn't interested.

Jacob Thompson
(Library of Congress photo)

Beverly Tucker
(Library of Congress photo)

Weeks later, according to researchers Balsiger and Sellier, Booth learned that his wife had been arrested in Tennessee for smuggling medical supplies to Confederate soldiers. Recalling Browning's earlier offer, he sought an audience with him. After informing Browning of his predicament, the secretary made arrangements for Booth to meet with Vice President Andrew Johnson. Johnson, in turn, told Booth that he could easily arrange for the release of his wife but he wanted something in return—the actor's help in re-establishing peace negotiations.

Booth agreed and told the vice president he would need passes to travel to Richmond as well as passes signed by Confederate authorities in order to return. Johnson, smiling, agreed.

Weeks later Booth returned from Richmond in a rage. He confronted Browning and, furious, told him that while he was in the South he learned that the papers found on Dahlgren were not forgeries, and that the intent had been to kill Davis and destroy Richmond all along.

Browning tried to pacify the irate actor, but Booth's anger was palpable and he accused the vice president's secretary of lying and deceit.

Fuming, Booth turned and strode away from Browning, an intense anger smoldering in his breast. He felt betrayed and used by the man he thought he could trust. Rather than cooling off, the anger and fury continued to burn, slowly at first, but soon with an intensity that gradually consumed the young actor.

On 9 August 1864 the Democratic National Convention made preparations to nominate General George McClellan to run against Lincoln. Booth, according to researchers Balsiger and Sellier, followed the progress of the convention closely and wrote in his journal that he believed the election of McClellan would help to bring the war to an end.

George B. McClellan
(National Archives photo)

Around this time, Booth was growing convinced that his service and contribution as a spy and as an occasional smuggler of medicines and bandages to the Southern camps was not enough—he wanted to do more and craved greater participation. Like others, Booth often entertained the notion of kidnapping the president.

Balsiger and Sellier discovered that during the final week of September 1864, planter Patrick Martin sought and received a meeting with John Wilkes Booth. At the time, Martin outlined a workable kidnap plot and discussed with Booth the possibilities of what might happen should McClellan be elected.

Martin also informed Booth that an adequate amount of gold would be made available for recruiting the right men for the job. He further convinced the actor that he would be generously compensated for his efforts. Martin also assured Booth that he could expect cooperation from the highest levels of the Confederate government in Richmond.

Booth told Martin he would give some thought to the proposition, and that he might even draft a letter of inquiry to President Jefferson Davis.

Edwin McMasters Stanton, President Lincoln's secretary of war, was by all accounts a strange man. Judged by today's standards, according to author Theodore Roscoe, Stanton would likely be considered psychotic. Once, on

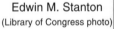

Edwin M. Stanton
(Library of Congress photo)

learning that a young woman he was fond of died from cholera, Stanton went to the cemetery and dug up her body, stating that he was afraid she had been buried alive. Several years later when Stanton's own daughter died and was buried, he had her corpse exhumed, placed in a different casket, and kept in his bedroom!

Stanton was born in Ohio in 1814. When he was thirteen years of age his father died and the family was thrust into financial difficulties. Life was difficult for young Stanton, but in 1831 he was able to enroll at Kenyon College and remain until his money was depleted two-and-a-half years later. He read law on his own and was finally admitted to the bar in 1836. He soon won a reputation as a competent and efficient attorney.

According to one writer, Stanton was "bellicose," "unfit," "apt to lose his head" in moments of stress, and was prone to "savage moods." It was said Stanton was unable to retain his composure long enough to form rational and equitable judgements, and Dewitt stated he would "boil over with rage whenever the course of affairs did not run to his liking."

In his memoirs, Ulysses Grant said of Stanton: "He cared nothing for the feelings of others. In fact, it seemed pleasanter to him to disappoint than gratify. He felt no hesitation in assuming the function of [President Lincoln] or in acting without advising him."

Stanton made no secret of his dislike for Abraham Lincoln. When he first met him, Stanton, then a noted lawyer, treated the young Abe Lincoln as though he were a mere bumpkin, refused to dine with him, and called him a "long-legged ape." After Lincoln was elected president, Stanton referred to him as an "imbecile," a "gorilla," and a "giraffe."

On 5 October 1864 a Confederate prisoner, Captain James William Boyd, was transferred from Hilton Head, South Carolina, to the Old Capitol Prison in Washington, a move specifically ordered by Secretary of War Stanton.

Boyd had enlisted in the Rebel army two years earlier and, as a result of oft-demonstrated competence and leadership, was soon given the responsibility of overseeing Confederate secret service operations in Western Tennessee. Eventually, Boyd was transferred to Virginia where he served in the same capacity. He was ultimately identified and captured by the National Detective Police in August 1863, formally charged with spying, and sent to the provost marshal's stockade in Memphis where he was subjected to intensive questioning for weeks.

During his incarceration, Boyd learned that his wife, who was living in Tennessee with their seven children, was sick and probably dying. He agreed to cooperate with the NDP if he would be released for a specified time and allowed to visit his ailing spouse. A deal was made: Using Boyd's sick wife as leverage, the Federals convinced the Confederate secret service captain to join the Union side.

Boyd was placed on the Federal payroll and given the responsibility of reporting on Confederate prisoners' escape plans. He was moved often and may have spent time in as many as five different prisons as an undercover agent. Shortly after being sent to Port Lookout, Maryland, an old ankle wound on his right leg developed a severe infection. In need of having it drained and treated, he arranged for a transfer to Hammond General Hospital on 20 May 1864.

While incarcerated at the Old Capitol Prison, Boyd learned his wife had died. He wrote a letter to Stanton requesting a transfer to Tennessee where, he said, he was willing to serve as a spy. He informed Stanton of the death of his wife. He also wrote that his seven children were living on charity and he wished to be near them.

On the day after receiving Boyd's letter, Stanton had the spy brought to his quarters. There, the secretary of war told him he would be freed if he would accept an important assignment. After listening to Stanton explain what he wanted accomplished, Boyd agreed to the duty—he was to kidnap President Abraham Lincoln!

James William Boyd was forty-three years old. According to Balsiger and Sellier, he was "slightly above average height" and possessed "wavy, reddish-brown hair and a scraggly moustache."

Facially, Boyd bore a remarkable resemblance to John Wilkes Booth.

The two men also shared the same initials.

Weeks after his meeting with Martin, Booth finally convinced himself he should contact Jefferson Davis and sent him a letter via courier. As a gesture of good faith, he also shipped 1,000 ounces of quinine to the Confederate hospital at Richmond.

Booth eventually received instructions to travel to Montreal. On 18 October he checked into St. Lawrence Hall and met with Clement Clay and Jacob Thompson. Clay was currently serving as a senator for the Confederate States of America and was involved in the secret peace negotiations. Thompson was now the head of the Confederate secret service in Canada. On arriving at the St. Lawrence, Booth was surprised to discover the hotel was swarming with Southern agents and politicians.

During a breakfast meeting with Clay and Thompson, Booth was told the South could certainly use his help if he were willing to undertake a dangerous assignment—the kidnapping of Abraham Lincoln. They agreed to allow the actor to select fifteen trusted men and provided him with $20,000 in gold to cover recruitment expenses. Thompson suggested Booth contact a man named John H. Surratt Jr. for help in organizing a force capable of completing the job.

Booth accepted the assignment, and Thompson informed him he was now part of the Confederate secret service. He was even provided the uniform of a Confederate colonel, which he placed in his trunk.

A short time later Booth returned to Washington. Within one week, the $20,000 in gold promised by Thompson was clandestinely delivered to him by a messenger from the Union's judge advocate general's office!

Now, with the financial resources and the authority to undertake the mission, Booth began making earnest plans to kidnap the president.

While Booth was outlining his approach to take Lincoln, a second plot to kidnap the president, as well as the vice president and the secretary of state, was being discussed and formulated by members of Lincoln's own party. Their intention was to make the abduction appear to be a Rebel scheme, and their aim was to imprison the abductees in the basement of the Washington mansion of Thomas Green, brother-in-law to Confederate general L.L. Lomax. While the president was shackled, fake charges of treason were to be filed and impeachment procedures undertaken.

On or about 1 November Booth was in New York and, using some of the money provided by Thompson and Clay, purchased carbines, revolvers, cartridges, belts, canteens, and handcuffs. All of these items were stored in a Washington boardinghouse owned and operated by Mary Surratt, mother of John.

By early November, National Detective Police adjutant William R. Bernard learned about Booth's plan to kidnap

Lincoln from a number of informants and federal spies and immediately informed Stanton. The secretary of war decided to wait and see how the plot developed and perhaps make an attempt to capture Booth and his accomplices. With careful planning, they considered, they might also nab some high-ranking Confederate officials.

One of the Union's principal informants was Captain James William Boyd, currently residing at the Old Capitol Prison. The prison was located just beyond the east grounds of the capitol. The building was once occupied by the U.S. Congress until 1819 and thereafter was referred to as the Old Capitol. When Congress was moved to newer quarters it was turned into a boardinghouse for senators and representatives. When the War Between the States broke out, it became a military prison.

It is believed Boyd learned of Booth's plans from Rebel inmates during the course of his normal duties as a prison spy. Little did he or anyone else know at the time, that the Confederate officer was soon to become deeply and inextricably involved in the tragic events of the future.

In late November, according to George S. Bryan, Booth traveled into southern Maryland to Bryantown where he presented a letter of introduction from Patrick Martin to Dr. William Queen. Booth reputedly suggested to Queen that he might be interested in purchasing some land in Charles County.

Queen introduced the actor to a number of residents, including Dr. Samuel A. Mudd. Mudd, thirty-one, owned a prosperous farm in Charles County, a farm inherited from his father and one to which he devoted a great deal of time working while he plied a small medical practice. Mudd took Booth on a tour of the nearby countryside and introduced him to other residents. During the tour, Booth purchased an old, one-eyed bay saddle horse from one of Mudd's neighbors.

Mudd and Booth met once again in Washington on 23 December. During this visit, the two men were walking toward the H Street boardinghouse of Mary Surratt when they happened to encounter her son, John Surratt, in the company of Louis Weichmann, one of Mrs. Surratt's boarders. Mudd introduced Booth to Surratt.

Dr. Samuel A. Mudd
(Library of Congress photo)

Booth and Surratt, after exchanging conversation and philosophies relative to the present political administration, agreed to begin recruiting a kidnap force. Booth was overjoyed to find Surratt eager to participate in the project.

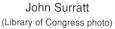

John Surratt
(Library of Congress photo)

Weichmann was a government employee and self-appointed informant. As he gradually learned about the plot to kidnap the president, he passed information on to Captain D.H.L. Gleason, a war department officer.

During his current stay in Washington, D.C., Booth often visited a shooting gallery to practice his marksmanship. Close friends remarked that Booth was an excellent shot.

Booth soon made a trip to Richmond where he met with former Louisiana senator Judah Benjamin. Benjamin had served, at various times, as Confederate attorney general, secretary of state, and secretary of war. Benjamin introduced Booth to Confederate vice president Alexander Stephens, and together the three men went to see President

Jefferson Davis. Davis provided Booth with a $70,000 draft and asked him if he would use it to arrange the movement of Southern cotton to Northern speculators and Northern meat to the armies of the South.

Benjamin arranged a meeting between Booth and bankers Jay and Henry Cooke in Philadelphia. The two financiers introduced Booth to several other men—senators, political bosses, lawyers, and cotton brokers. As the conversation progressed, it became increasingly clear to Booth that many of Lincoln's close friends and presumed allies were speculating in cotton and gold with the South. Among them, according to information uncovered by Balsiger and Sellier, was Lincoln's trusted friend, Ward Lamon!

Lamon, who was responsible for obtaining Lincoln's signatures on numerous documents during the course of a week, told those assembled that it was a small matter getting the president to sign cotton passes. Lincoln, he said, seldom looked at what he was signing.

Booth later recorded an entry in his diary relative to the fact that each of the men at this meeting had business dealings with the Confederate States of America and, as long as a profit could be made, would continue to do so.

Booth asked the men how he could be of service. In response, Jay Cooke handed him two letters, both written in code, and asked the actor to deliver them to Confederate agents Beverly Tucker and Jacob Thompson in Montreal. Booth took the letters and left for Canada.

As Booth was signing the register at St. Lawrence Hall for the second time, he was startled to see Confederate agent Nathaniel Beverly Tucker leaving the hotel in the company of Lafayette Baker, chief of the National Detective Police, the United State's precursor to the Secret Service. Booth went immediately to the room of Confederate agent George N. Sanders and reported what he saw.

Sanders excused himself and returned several minutes later with Tucker. Booth, uncomfortable not knowing what was going on, listened in silence as the two men spoke with one another. Presently, Canadian Secret Service chief Jacob Thompson arrived carrying a black leather satchel. Booth eventually produced the coded letters from his coat pocket and gave one each to Thompson and Tucker.

After the letters were decoded, Thompson handed Booth the satchel and told him it contained $50,000 in bank notes and $15,000 in cash, all of which was to be delivered to California senator John Conness. There was an additional $20,000 to be delivered to Senator Benjamin Wade, a staunch critic of McClellan and close friend of Secretary of War Stanton! The rest of the money, explained Thompson, was to be used by Booth for recruiting men.

Booth returned to Washington with the satchel, deeply confused yet exhilarated at the promise of adventure and notoriety. Delighted to be involved in advancing the cause of the South, Booth was nevertheless amazed at the machinations and deceptions of the Washington politicians.

On 11 December Ward Lamon repeated his warning to the president that his life was in danger and that he needed to take more precautions against kidnap or assassination. Lincoln, however, continued to attend the theater with little or no provision for his safety.

Lincoln truly enjoyed the theater, and at the time Washington had several: Grover's on Pennsylvania Avenue; Canterbury Music Hall; Oxford Hall; Seaton Hall; and the most popular, Ford's Theater on Tenth Street.

Along with others, Major Thomas Eckert, an aide to Stanton, also received information of Booth's role in the kidnap plot. Eventually, Lincoln was provided with an armed escort of cavalrymen when he went on trips. William B. Webb, the Washington chief of police, appointed four officers to guard the president. The men—Alphonso Dunn, John Parker, Thomas Pendel, and Alexander Smith—were all armed with revolvers and ordered to "stand between the president and danger" at all times.

John Parker was an odd choice to guard the president. Formerly with the Metropolitan Police, he was a known malcontent and during his brief service had been twice charged with conduct unbecoming an officer, willful violation of police regulations, sleeping on duty, using offensive language, insubordination, and visiting a brothel. Parker, like Boyd, was destined to play a significant role in future events.

According to Balsiger and Sellier, Booth, on returning to Washington, delivered the packets of money to Conness and Wade. During his meeting with Conness, the senator told him he was aware of the plans to kidnap the president and suggested he could be of some assistance. He also told Booth that not only should the president be abducted, but also the vice president and the secretary of state. Booth expressed surprise at this development and asked why, but Conness only told him the reasons were to remain confidential for the time being.

Booth reasoned that Conness was in league with the Radical Republicans who wanted to control the government and exploit the South. He was also well aware that Conness had a great deal of money at his disposal. Booth did not particularly like the planters because their goal in removing Lincoln was profit motivated. Conness' plan, determined Booth, would go a long way in bargaining for the release of Confederate prisoners. Booth actually cared little for Conness and even less for his politics, but he agreed to cooperate and asked the senator how he planned to help.

Conness replied that he and his accomplices were quite intimate with the daily schedules and movements of the men targeted for kidnap. Booth was told that if all three could not be abducted, the president must be the first. At the time, Booth was completely unaware of the Radicals' plan to seize control of the executive branch, control reconstruction, prevent the Democrats from dominating Congress, and to "deny inauguration to Southern-leaning McClellan."

So convinced was Booth that Conness' plan could be successful that he began enlisting the help of others. He quickly recruited two of his boyhood friends—Samuel Bland Arnold and Michael O'Laughlin. Arnold was a class-

Samuel Bland Arnold
(Library of Congress photo)

mate of Booth's at St. Timothy's, and Booth had known O'Laughlin while living at Belair. Both men had served as Confederate soldiers, and O'Laughlin once assisted Booth in smuggling quinine and other medicines into the South.

Booth explained to his two friends that he planned to kidnap Lincoln and exchange him for Confederate prisoners, and he outlined his plan in detail for them. Actually he had two plans, each based on opportunity. One would be to capture the president on the road during one of his visits to the theater at the Soldiers Home, located three miles from the White House. The other plan, perhaps the better of the two, would be to grab Lincoln while he was attending a play at Ford's Theater.

Booth also acquired the services of David Herold and George Atzerodt. Herold was an unemployed youth of about twenty-three years of age who lived with his widowed mother and seven sisters. He had no particular skills other than that he knew many of the roads of Washington and southern Maryland. Herold had once worked as a clerk in a drug store but was currently unemployed. He spent most of his days wandering the streets of Washington and most of his nights standing around outside the theaters. Herold, though an adult, was far more of a boy than a man. Family friends referred to him as a "callow boy" and a bit of a "simpleton." He has been described by researcher Dewitt as "light and trifling," "unreliable," and easily manipulated. During his trial subsequent to his capture, Herold was referred to as having the mind of an eleven-year-old boy.

Atzerodt, a German immigrant, worked as a carriage painter in a coach-making shop established by his brother John at Port Tobacco. He owned a boat, which he kept there and sometimes used to ferry Southerners bound to and

David Herold
(Library of Congress photo)

George Atzerodt
(Library of Congress photo)

from Richmond across the Potomac. Atzerodt was a rough-looking, solid man, who spoke in a heavy German accent. According to writer Dewitt, he was "fierce in appearance and talk, but cowardly at heart." He is described by Roscoe as "earthy," a "clod," a "lout," "crude," and ate with his knife.

With the recruitment of Herold and Atzerodt, Booth studied a number of potential escape routes. After rejecting several possibilities, he settled on a flight across the Navy Yard Bridge that crossed the Potomac River at the end of Eleventh Street. Once decided on this route, he then planned several alternative ones.

Booth then recruited Edman "Ned" Spangler, a sometime stagehand, sceneshifter, and carpenter at Ford's

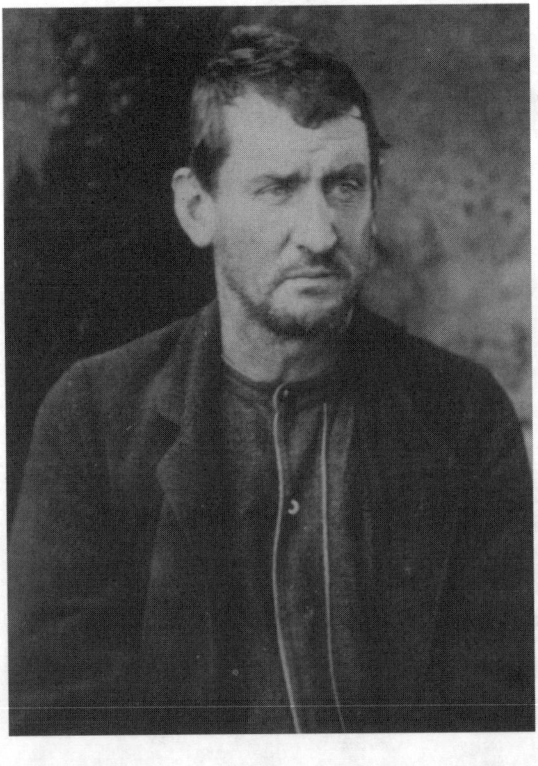

Edman "Ned" Spangler
(Library of Congress photo)

Theater who groomed Booth's horse and who once worked for the Booth family. Spangler has been described by Roscoe as a "composite of ignorance, incompetence, poverty, sloth, turpitude, distemper, and alcoholism . . . . " Should Booth decide to snatch Lincoln while he was attending a play, Spangler would be a valuable asset—he could control the lights and, as he knew the stage, could help transport the president through the dark. It is believed Booth paid Spangler off in drinks.

Booth also recruited Lewis Paine (sometimes spelled Payne). Paine, according to some researchers, was one of several aliases used by Lewis Thornton Powell, once a Confederate soldier who served with Mosby's Raiders. Other

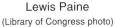

Lewis Paine
(Library of Congress photo)

aliases included Reverend, Wood, Hull, Kincheloe, and Mosby.

Paine (Powell) was from Tallahassee, Florida, the son a Baptist preacher, one of nine children, and known to be a hard-shell fundamentalist and an avowed racist. Roscoe stated Paine had the strength of a giant and the "instincts of a panther."

Paine fought at Antietam, Chancellorsville, Richmond, and Gettysburg. He was wounded at Gettysburg, taken prisoner, escaped, and rejoined the Rebel army. In January 1865 Paine, after losing two brothers at Murfreesboro, made his way to Alexandria where he took an oath of allegiance to the United States.

In spite of what many researchers describe as his coarse ways, Paine was a fan of the theater and would attend performances when he could afford a ticket. The first time he ever saw a play was one evening while he was stationed in Richmond. John Wilkes Booth was the featured actor and made a lasting impression on the young man. Following the performance, Paine initiated a conversation with Booth, and the two men, so different in so many ways, became friends.

Paine later arrived in Washington. He was homeless, penniless, and dressed in rags, but he was taken in by Booth who provided him with food, clothing, and money.

Paine was tall, heavily muscled, and extremely strong. Coarse black hair was parted low on the left side of his head, his eyes were dark, and his complexion ruddy. It has been concluded by a number of researchers that Paine was deranged.

Not only had Booth given Paine money and a place to live, he had provided the former Confederate with a plan whereby he could exact revenge on the hated Yankees. In

Booth's scenario, the muscular Paine would be strong enough to carry Lincoln.

Ultimately, the members of Booth's kidnap conspiracy included Arnold, Atzerodt, Herold, O'Laughlin, Paine, and John Surratt. In addition to these men, it is believed, he received promises of aid from Dr. William T. Bowman, John C. Thompson, Samuel Cox, and Thomas Jones.

On learning of the cast of characters in Booth's production, Weichmann provided their names, along with that of Mary Surratt, to Captain Gleason. He also specified that the plotters intended to spirit Lincoln out of Washington by way of the Navy Yard Bridge. Gleason immediately relayed this information to Army Intelligence Headquarters in the War Department, but they ignored it.

Weichmann's motives for spying on the conspirators and reporting on the clandestine activities of Booth and his comrades have long been debated. Some refer to him merely as a patriotic and concerned citizen. Others point to the fact that Weichmann once attempted to court Mary Surratt's daughter, Anna, who also resided in the boardinghouse. Anna, however, was infatuated with the charming and dashing John Wilkes Booth. Once, while Weichmann was conversing with Anna in the parlor of the boardinghouse, she became offended at something he said and slapped him hard across the face. At least one historian has concluded that the rebuffed Weichmann sought vengeance against Booth and the Surratts as a result of his rejection by the girl.

Booth began to enjoy his role as leader of the kidnap plot. He could envision himself a hero in the abduction of the president of the United States and the ultimate release of Confederate prisoners. His actor's ego swelled at the possibilities of fame far greater than what the stage could ever deliver. His craving for recognition, for notoriety burned within, and he continued to feed the fires.

Booth had played Ford's Theater on many occasions. For several afternoons in a row during December 1864, he entered the building and began an intense study of how the kidnapping should progress. He determined that, once the lights were lowered, Lincoln would be grabbed in his private box, his hands cuffed, lowered to the stage, carried bodily out into the alley, placed in a carriage, and spirited toward the Navy Yard Bridge and Maryland. Despite oft-expressed discouragement from his co-conspirators, particularly Arnold and O'Laughlin. Booth was convinced such a plan could work. Rather than becoming discouraged by the others, he grew even more excited and eager.

David Herold was given the responsibility of assembling a team of horses to be used as a relay, if necessary, on the southern bank of the Anacostia River near the Navy Yard Bridge.

John Surratt was sent to tell Atzerodt at Port Tobacco to have a flatboat at the ready to receive the carriage bearing the kidnapped president.

Booth gathered materials he believed necessary to carry out the plot—handcuffs, ropes, and a gag—and arranged to have them stored in a room at the National Hotel. He also provided for a carriage to be pulled up in the alley next to the stage door at a signal from one of the recruits.

As the plan evolved, Booth decided he and Surratt, on the dimming of the house lights, would enter the presidential box, grab Lincoln, gag and handcuff him, then lower him to the stage. From there, he was to be lifted by Paine and rushed out the backstage door and transported into Maryland. Booth decided the evening of 18 January 1865 was the best time to take the president.

Men and equipment were readied, and minute by minute the tension mounted. That night, however, it rained and stormed and Lincoln chose not to attend the theater.

During the first week of March 1865, Booth was stunned to discover he was being removed as the leader of the plot to kidnap the president. His sources informed him he had been replaced by a Confederate officer now in league with the Union. The following morning, Booth met with James V. Barnes, speculator and cotton broker, and vented his frustrations.

Booth was outraged at his dismissal as leader of the plot. His chance for glory was gone, vanished, and his actor's ego was reeling at the cancellation. After all the work he had invested in the plan, to be treated in such a manner made him furious. Booth exploded at Barnes, pacing and screaming and telling him repeatedly that he refused to be replaced. He claimed that the entire plot was his own creation, a product of his investment of time, energy, and money, and that he refused to step down as leader.

Barnes, who stood to gain tremendously in cotton contracts if the Radical Republicans took over, told Booth there was nothing that could be done. He also stated that the Confederate States of America were going to fall and would be of no help.

Steaming with rage and anger, Booth cursed Barnes and Lincoln. Red-faced and furious, he stormed out of the room. John Wilkes Booth's hatred for the president now grew in intensity such that it twisted his face in rage and anguish.

Though Booth tried on several occasions to learn the identity of the man who had been assigned to replace him as the leader of the kidnap plot, he was unsuccessful.

26
29

It was Captain James William Boyd.

In front of others, Booth tried to pretend that his removal was not affecting him. From some of his own well-placed spies, he learned that the new leader planned to take Lincoln, not to Richmond as the actor planned, but to Bloodsworth Island in the Chesapeake Bay where he was to be killed by Union agents.

Booth seethed because everything had been taken away from him. He now believed it imperative that he get to the president before the others. He saw it as his duty, and he would not give up. He was determined not to allow this chance at eternal fame to be snatched away from him.

By February, things were not going well for the South. The Confederates were losing their last vital Southern port at Wilmington, North Carolina. After burning, looting, and destroying a significant portion of the state of Georgia, General William Tecumseh Sherman was doing the same in South Carolina on his way to North Carolina. The Confederate command of Jubal Early was about to be wiped out by General Philip Sheridan, and Grant was threatening Richmond.

On 4 March Lincoln was sworn in as president for his second term, the inaugural festivities held in the eastern portico of the Capitol Building. John Wilkes Booth, having obtained a pass from New Hampshire senator John Hale, was present at the ceremony.

After being given the oath of office by Chief Justice Salmon P. Chase, Lincoln gave his address. As the president spoke, Booth managed to gain a position immediately above and behind him, looking down on Lincoln as he completed his address.

According to Benn Pittman in *The Assassination of President Lincoln and the Trial of the Conspirators*, Booth proclaimed to a friend several days later that he'd had "an elegant chance . . . to kill the president . . . if I wished."

By March, Captain James William Boyd had returned from Canada where he met and reviewed plans with several ranking officials. After moving into a residence in Maryland, he began preparations to implement the plan he had been assigned to carry out. Relative to his mission, Boyd discreetly made inquiries about specific routes and roads. During this time, the wound in his right ankle was giving him trouble—it was not healing properly and forced Boyd to move about on crutches.

Booth determined that the plot to kidnap the president was still viable, and he continued to curse the circumstances that led to his dismissal. With bruised ego and growing anger, he began hatching a plan of his own, a plan he was convinced would catapult him ahead of his rivals, a plan that would make him known to the world.

Booth's new kidnap plot began to take shape during the second week of March. He decided he would grab the president at Grover's Theater on the evening of 15 March. On 13 March, however, the actor read in the newspaper that Lincoln was very ill. Booth presumed the president would be unable to attend the theater, so he cancelled the preparations. As it turned out, however, Lincoln recovered sufficiently to go to Grover's Theater.

The next day, Booth summoned O'Laughlin, Surratt, and Paine and informed them of his latest plan. According to Balsiger and Sellier, he arranged for Paine and Surratt, accompanied by their dates, to attend the performance of *Jane Shore* at Ford's Theater on the evening of 15 March.

The tickets were for seats in the presidential box. During intermission, Booth visited his accomplices, and together they thoroughly examined the configuration, layout, ingresses, and egresses.

It is believed that while Booth was examining the theater, David Herold traveled to Surrattsville, about ten miles southeast of Washington in Prince Georges County, Maryland. Here, he went to Surratt's Tavern, owned by Mary Surratt, where he met with Atzerodt and John Surratt. Before leaving, the three men deposited a bundle of guns and other gear with proprietor John Lloyd who hid them in an upstairs room.

Late one evening several days later following a performance, Booth met with Arnold, Atzerodt, Herold, O'Laughlin, Paine, Surratt, and James Wood in a back room of Gautier's Restaurant. Booth unrolled a floor plan of Ford's Theater and explained his plan for kidnapping Lincoln during a production. Most of those attending were stunned at the sheer boldness of the plot and voiced concern that it was too dangerous and unrealistic and had little or no chance for success. Surratt argued that the government was aware of a plot to kidnap the president and suggested the plan be dropped for the time being.

At this Booth's ego took another blow. He was still reeling as a result of being replaced as leader of the Northern kidnap plot, and he was determined to get to the president before his replacement.

Booth was also infuriated with the lack of cooperation he was getting from his fellow conspirators and even angrier that they dared question his decisions. He was gradually losing control not only of his accomplices, but of himself.

The following morning, it was learned that Lincoln was to attend a play at 2:00 P.M. at the Seventh Street Hospital, entertainment that was designed for the wounded soldiers being treated there. The skies had been growing dark and menacing all day, the wind was picking up, and the temperature dropping rapidly.

Booth, accompanied by Arnold, Atzerodt, Herold, O'Laughlin, Paine, Surratt, and Wood were mounted and riding toward the hospital by 1:30 P.M. All were armed. They pulled up in a grove of trees adjacent to a curve in the road, and from this vantage point, they could observe the approach of anyone traveling toward the hospital.

According to Roscoe, Booth, accompanied by Surratt, would ride out into the road in front of the presidential carriage when it came around the curve. The rest of the conspirators were to assume a position behind the carriage. Surratt was to grab the coachman, divest him of his clothes, and put them on himself. Arnold, Atzerodt, Herold, O'Laughlin, and Wood were to occupy the cavalry escort while Booth and Paine cuffed and gagged Lincoln.

As the men awaited the presidential carriage, a hard sleet began to fall. Sitting astride their horses, they were growing cold and uncomfortable and anxious for something to happen. Presently, the sound of an approaching carriage was heard, and each man tensed as they waited in silence. Suddenly, Booth and Surratt spurred their mounts out into the road and were quickly followed by the others who took positions behind the vehicle. As he peered into the carriage, Booth was startled to discover its occupant was not Lincoln at all, but Secretary of the Treasury Salmon P. Chase.

Foiled again, the conspirators fled. Like the previous two kidnap attempts, the third was a failure. Booth learned the next day that Lincoln had been attending a ceremony at the National Hotel where he presented a battle flag to the governor of Indiana.

Shortly after the third failed kidnap attempt, Arnold and O'Laughlin decided to leave Booth. They were growing concerned that the actor's expanding ego and somewhat loose and overzealous approach to abducting the president would get them all in trouble. They told him they believed the plan was a losing proposition and recommended he abandon it. Booth did not listen to the advice from his two friends, and he pursued his scheme with renewed vigor.

According to Balsiger and Sellier, Booth and his remaining conspirators made yet a fourth attempt to kidnap the president. Unfortunately for them, Lincoln was surrounded by a contingent of armed cavalry. It was Booth's fourth setback.

On 19 March, Booth was given some information on Lincoln's movements by Conness. Gathering his associates, the actor rode to a predetermined location to await the passage of the president, but Lincoln never appeared.

Frustrated and angered by the unaccustomed failures, Booth grew increasingly discouraged and began drinking more than normal. He was often seen in Taltavul's, a restaurant and saloon adjoining Ford's Theater, drinking large amounts of brandy and growing irascible and humorless.

On the morning of 20 March, Booth received word about another movement. He quickly assembled his men and, hidden among some trees, waited for the president at a selected ambush site. As they lay concealed some distance away from a road, word was delivered to Booth that the ambush plan was known to the authorities. They fled, and Booth was certain he was being set up.

During the next few days as he fumed over this sixth failure, Booth found fault with everyone but himself and was certain someone was plotting his undoing. His suspicions eventually centered on Conness, a man he had distrusted from the beginning. Gradually, Booth convinced himself that Conness wanted him out of the picture altogether.

A few days later, Booth, armed with a carbine, accompanied by Paine and Surratt, and acting on information provided by an unknown source, took up a position in a grove of trees alongside a road a short distance from the White House. Presently a group of horsemen came cantering down the road. The three conspirators immediately recognized the president, who was surrounded by an armed escort. It is not clear whether the original intent of the conspirators was to kidnap or assassinate. It may be that the escort discouraged a kidnap attempt. In any event, Booth raised his rifle, aimed, and fired. The bullet struck Lincoln's hat, knocking it off. Paine fired twice, missing both times. Yet another failure.

Now Booth was not only becoming more frustrated, he was growing desperate. He was seeing his opportunities for fame and notoriety fading.

Balsiger and Sellier write that several days following the attempt on the president's life, Booth, in the company of Paine, was visited by Colonel Everton J. Conger. Conger told Booth he knew of his attempt to ambush the president, accused him of being reckless, and called him a fool. He reminded him that he had been dropped from the plot to kidnap the president.

Angrily, Booth informed Conger he was now acting on his own. The actor told his visitor that it was he, Booth, who had designed the plan to abduct the president, and that he intended to see it through. Conger responded by telling Booth in no uncertain terms that if he did not remove himself from the scene that he and his friends would be eliminated.

On 2 April, Petersburg was taken by the Union army, and Richmond was only hours away from falling. Booth fumed—his original plan and motives for kidnapping the president were now completely useless. While meeting with the speculators in New York, Booth blamed National Detective Police commander Lafayette Baker. Booth insisted that once the South had fallen, Baker would likely betray the businessmen, arrest them, perhaps even have them killed. He insisted something must be done, and soon. The speculators told him to return to Washington and await further orders.

Lafayette Baker bothered Booth. Named by Stanton to be chief of the nation's Secret Service, Baker established offices in the Treasury Building and, with help from the

Lafayette C. Baker
(Library of Congress photo)

secretary of war, formed an army of some 2,000 secret agents and developed a sophisticated intelligence network.

Though a relatively unknown historical figure to most Americans, Baker is regarded by scholars as one of the more powerful Union figures who worked behind the scenes during the Civil War. Baker was thirty-eight years old, average height, slender, with gray eyes and a full beard. He never drank alcohol and never used profane language. He was considered a superb horseman and an expert marksman. Baker was regarded even by his foremost detractors as an excellent detective.

Baker was also egotistical, ambitious, and considered by most to be entirely untrustworthy. As chief of the NDP, he introduced for the first time in America's law enforcement history the concepts of midnight raids, entry without warrant, summary arrests, and imprisonment without bail. Baker's NDP was also credited with unbridled corruption, including bribery and blackmail. Baker himself was known to lie, cheat, and employ whatever means necessary to accomplish his goals. It has been written that many hated Baker for his deception and intimidating practices.

On 9 April, Lee surrendered to Grant at Appomattox. The war was now over. Booth was stricken with this news. According to Balsiger and Sellier, he was convinced the politicians would "strip the South bare." He lamented in his diary that all "we have planned and striven for has come for naught . . . I believe Eckert, [Colonel Lafayette C.] Baker and the Secretary [Stanton] are in control of our activities."

Booth was convinced that Stanton believed removing Lincoln would assure his remaining in office as secretary of war. With the war over, Stanton would be concerned Lincoln might not need him any longer. Booth believed that if

Stanton remained in office and was placed in charge of reconstruction and military government of the South, he would become the most powerful man in the country. As the nation's most influential man, Stanton stood an excellent chance of eventually being elected to the presidency. The faithful Eckert, Stanton's assistant and chief of the War Department telegraph office, would most assuredly accompany Stanton in his rise to power.

Baker would likewise advance his prestige in government, since he would be in charge of secret service operations in the South as well as the North. Though essentially unknown to the American public, one of Baker's chief duties was the protection of the president.

Booth was nervous because he knew Baker was aware of his plans to abduct Lincoln, and the actor was not certain whether Baker would be friend or foe.

CHAPTER IV

Plot To Assassinate

On 10 April, Lafayette Baker sought an audience with Stanton and told him he had obtained information of a plot to assassinate the president. The information was based on secret ciphers provided by Major Thomas T. Eckert. Eckert, in charge of Federal ciphers, had years of experience decoding Confederate messages.

Baker told Stanton that the attempt was to take place on 14 April. Stanton, however, told Baker he did not believe the information was accurate and dismissed him immediately.

The next day, Stanton called Baker back into his office and told him he was in possession of information that linked him, Baker, to the assassination plot. Baker, of course, denied it.

The following morning, Baker met with NDP agent Earl Potter and told him he believed Stanton was insane and hated Lincoln. Baker stated that he was convinced Stanton was ultimately responsible for the assassination plot that had recently been uncovered. He also expressed the concern that, if it happened, he, Baker, would be blamed for it.

Booth, broken by the surrender of the South, was now deeply concerned for his own safety and may have feared for his life. Quoting from the missing pages of Booth's diary, researchers Balsiger and Sellier claimed the actor wrote that he was now determined to kill the president and that he "shall lay the body of this tyrant dead upon the altar of [Stanton]. If by this act, I am slain, they too shall be cast into hell, for I have given information to a friend who will have the nation know who the traitors are."

A short time later Booth received another message from the New York speculators. After reading it, he made an entry in his diary that mentioned a new plan. More importantly, he was to be "in charge."

On the morning of 12 April, Booth was seen in Deery's Saloon drinking heavily, one brandy after another.

That evening, President Lincoln delivered a speech from the Executive Mansion in which he promised citizenship for the freed slaves. In the audience were Booth and David Herold. Booth, enraged at the president's message, turned to Herold and stated, "That means nigger citizenship. Now, by God, I'll put him through."

He returned to Deery's and, as was now his pattern, drank more.

Captain James William Boyd was keeping busy acquiring riding stock in Prince Georges County, Maryland. During this undertaking, Boyd learned that a retired Confederate officer named Thomas H. Watkins attempted to rape the wife of one of his close friends. Boyd took sudden leave of his duties to search for Watkins. When he found him, he shot him in the back of the head, killing him instantly. A soldier named John H. Boyle was blamed for the crime, but Boyd eventually confessed his guilt. (As a result of this mix-up, historians have long confused Boyd with Boyle). Though Boyd's superiors learned about the murder, they did nothing. His current assignment, they reasoned, was more important to them than having him arrested and tried for killing the soldier.

Booth continued to drink more and more, and the liquor appeared to fuel his Southern passions, which flared and sometimes exploded. He grew increasingly and visibly frustrated. He loudly blamed Lincoln for everything bad that was happening, and his hatred for the president only deepened.

On the afternoon of 13 April, Booth encountered a fellow actor named E.A. Emerson, and the two men spoke briefly about Lincoln and the surrender of the South. During the conversation, according to Emerson, Booth referred to Lincoln and stated, "Somebody ought to kill the old scoundrel."

On the morning of 14 April, John Wilkes Booth rose at 7:30 A.M. and breakfasted at the dining room of the National Hotel. Following his meal, he walked to a barbershop where he was shaved between 9:00 and 10:00 A.M. While at the barbershop he encountered Henry Johnson, his black valet, as well as O'Laughlin and Surratt. Afterward, Booth, O'Laughlin, and Surratt returned to the National Hotel, arriving around 10:30 A.M., where they conversed privately. According to a statement made later by O'Laughlin, Booth told him that the next time Lincoln attended a play at Ford's Theater, a soldier would enter his box during the intermission at the end of the second act and tell the president his presence was needed at the War Department. The guards, said Booth, will be lured away, drugged, and replaced by others friendly to the cause.

Outside the theater, Booth continued, the president will be placed in his carriage and escorted by a troop of cavalry to the homes of Secretary of State Seward and Vice President Johnson, both of whom would be forced to join Lincoln in the carriage. The carriage would then be led out of Washington to Maryland by way of the Navy Yard Bridge, through Surrattsville and Bryantown to Benedict's Landing on the Patuxent River, an arm of the Chesapeake Bay. There, the three were to be loaded onto an awaiting ship.

Booth, now excited and very animated, was revived by this plan, which he believed was daring, risky, dashing, and original. In his current state of mind, the actor envisioned himself a national hero.

Booth told O'Laughlin and Surratt that after the abduction the prisoners would be hidden at an unspecified location. Booth would then proceed to Europe where he had arranged for bank credits in England and France. He informed his two co-conspirators that he had made arrangements for a ship to pick him up at Port Tobacco and take him to the Bahamas. Six weeks following the abduction, he told them, arrangements would be made to have the two men rendezvous with him in England.

Booth excused himself from O'Laughlin and Surratt, went to the home of Mrs. Surratt, and visited with her for several minutes. It was Good Friday, and she was preparing to attend services at St. Patrick's Catholic Church. After leaving the boardinghouse, Booth walked to Ford's Theater, arriving just before noon.

Ford's Theater was a rather impressive three-story brick building located on Washington's Tenth Street. Originally a Baptist church, it had since been abandoned and neglected. In 1861 John T. Ford, a Baltimore producer, envisioned its possibilities as a theater and leased the

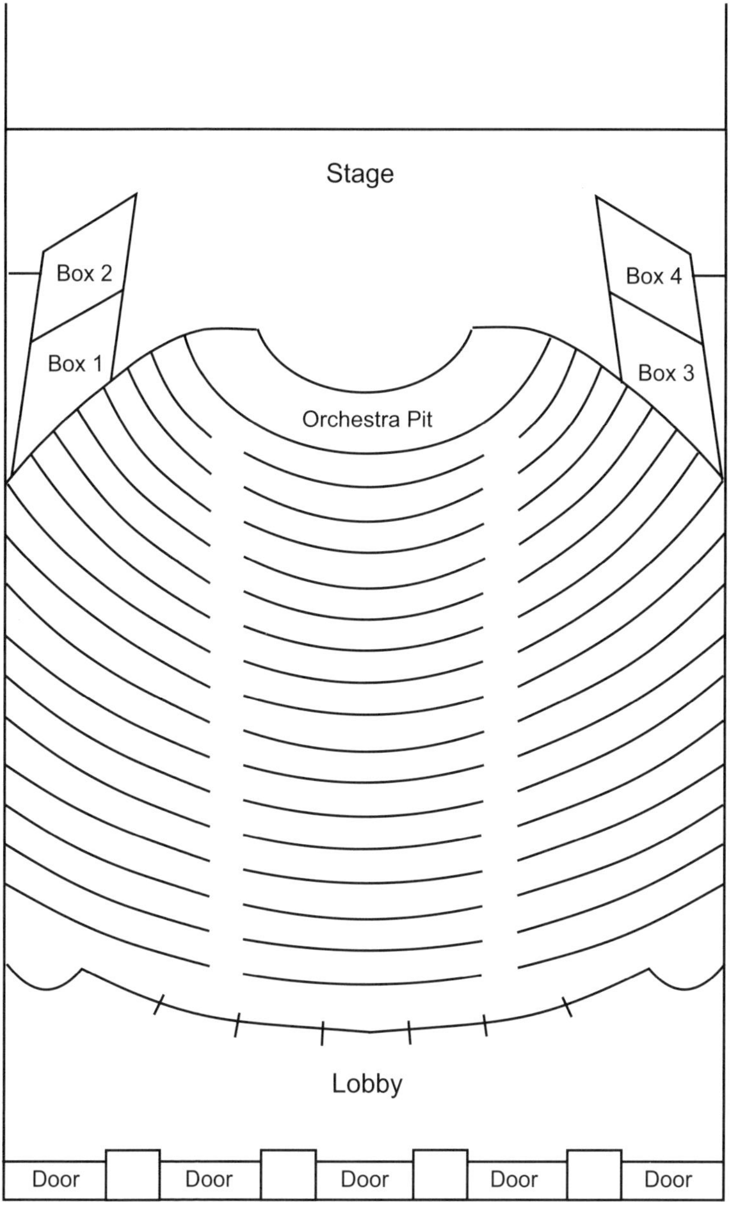

Orchestra and parquette seating (first floor) of Ford's Theater

building. It burned to the ground in December 1862, and Ford rebuilt it to his own specifications. Before long, it became one of Washington's most popular showplaces. Abraham Lincoln, seeking diversion from his heavy responsibilities, often attended dramatic productions at Ford's Theater.

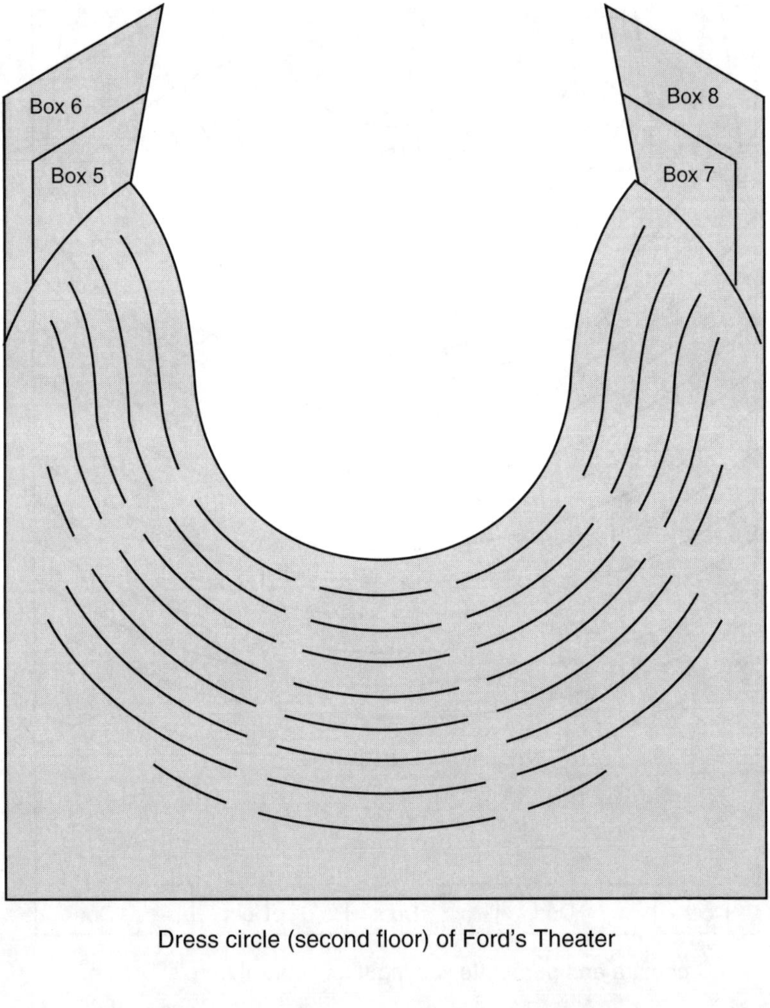

Dress circle (second floor) of Ford's Theater

Behind the theater was an alley, called "Baptist's Alley," which was approximately thirty feet wide. Two hundred yards away were some stables. Mrs. Mary J. Anderson, a black woman who lived in a dwelling that fronted the alley, testified later that she watched Booth walk through the alley and down to the stables where he kept a horse.

Booth entered the lobby of Ford's Theater to pick up his mail. Tom Raybold, a ticket salesman, handed the actor several letters and a package.

After reading his mail, Booth walked to the stables on C Street operated by James W. Pumphrey and rented a "small bay mare with a black mane and tail and white spot on her forehead." Pumphrey warned Booth that the mare was high-strung and sometimes snapped her bridle when hitched. Booth accepted the mare and told the stable owner he would return for her around 4:00 P.M.

While Booth was making arrangements to lease the horse, a messenger arrived at the theater's box office to make reservations for President Lincoln and a private party to watch that evening's performance of *Our American Cousin* starring Laura Keene, a prominent actress. The theater treasurer made the arrangements and told an employee to prepare the presidential box. He then made a poster containing the information that the president and his party would be attending that evening and placed it in the box office where it could be seen by passersby. This done, he hastily prepared newspaper ads and handbills which were distributed around town.

Around 1:00 P.M., Booth returned to Ford's Theater and spotted the poster and the information pertaining to the president's attendance. Excited, he turned and hastened to Deery's Saloon located in nearby Grover's Theater where he ordered a drink and drafted a letter to James C. Welling, the editor of the *National Intelligencer*. The letter, a copy of which Balsiger and Sellier located in a private collection belonging to Stanton's descendants, began with the sentence, "By the time you read this, I will either have accomplished my purpose or be myself beyond the reach of any man's hand." He also wrote of loving peace more than his own life. Toward the end of the letter, he wrote that Lincoln's acceptance of the blacks as citizens was preparing the way for "total annihilation," and that Lincoln's government "is the most corrupt in the nation's history." Booth also provided the names of thirty-five men whom he identified as wishing to "exploit the now bloody, defeated Southern states." The names included Lamon, several major senators, military officers, the Speaker of the House, judges, bankers, and businessmen. He folded the letter, placed it in his pocket, and departed.

Returning to the National Hotel, he went to his room, bathed, and then went to the Kirkwood House Hotel. There, he left a message for Vice President Johnson's secretary, Colonel Browning, and walked out. A few minutes later, Browning walked in, received the message, and went to his room. Learning that Browning had returned, Booth went back to the Kirkwood House and sent a bellhop to inform the secretary he awaited an audience with him, but the bellhop returned and curtly informed Booth that the secretary was not in.

Enraged at being refused an audience, Booth stormed out of the hotel. He went to a nearby saloon where he encountered an acquaintance named Ed Henson who invited him to have a drink.

Henson was a shadowy, rather elusive figure. Virtually all that is known of him prior to the assassination is that he was involved with Booth smuggling contraband into the South.

As the two drank whiskey, they lamented that with the war's end they would no longer have the opportunity to earn money as smugglers. Henson, who closely resembled David Herold but was somewhat older, told Booth that he was going to miss the excitement. Booth replied that the excitement was just about to begin and invited Henson to participate.

Booth left the saloon and went to a room at the Herndon House where he found Paine. He informed Paine something was in the works and told him it was important to meet back there that evening. He also told Paine a horse would be tied in the stable behind Ford's Theater.

At Ford's Theater, workmen were preparing the presidential box. During the mid-1800s, theater boxes were much different from the somewhat more spacious lodges of playhouses that were constructed years later. The boxes actually extended a bit over the stage and were separated from the rest of the auditorium not by curtains but by doors that could be locked.

The partitions between Ford's boxes seven and eight were removed and a sofa and three extra chairs were brought in. A fourth chair—a black walnut rocker with seat, arms, and back upholstered in red damask—was placed in the box next to the wall screening it from the balcony audience and approximately four feet from the door. The rocker was reserved for Lincoln, who would sit close to the audience and about twelve feet directly above the stage apron.

Access to the boxes could only be had via the south side of the second floor, and entry was through a single door that led into a small antechamber. Next to this door, a cane-bottomed chair was placed for a White House guard. Anyone wishing to reach Lincoln would have to pass by the guard.

Presidential box, Ford's Theater
(Library of Congress photo)

Across the front of the box, a U.S. treasury flag was draped. Centered just above the flag hung a picture of George Washington.

Many researchers believe that sometime during the day, Booth entered the president's box from which he observed the actors in rehearsal. Using a knife, he carved a small niche in the plaster wall just inside the corridor. This was to accommodate a length of wood that would be used to secure the door. Using a gimlet—a small tool with a screw point, grooved shank, and crossed handle used for boring holes—he reamed a tiny opening at eye level in the upper wooden panel of the door to the box. Looking through this hole, Booth would be able to see Lincoln's chair.

Around 2:30, Booth went to visit Mrs. Surratt once again at her boardinghouse. They conversed quietly for several minutes before she departed for church.

Approximately one hour later, Booth wrote several more letters. He eventually returned to Pumphrey's livery stable and obtained the bay horse he had selected earlier. Later, as he rode up Pennsylvania Avenue, he spotted John Matthews walking along the sidewalk. Matthews was an actor Booth earlier tried to enlist in one of his plots to kidnap the President. He handed Matthews the letter he wrote earlier to the editor of the *National Intelligencer* and asked him to deliver it. Matthews expressed confusion but agreed to do so. The letter was never published.

For the rest of the afternoon, Booth visited some of his regular haunts. At one point, he rode the bay mare up and down Pennsylvania Avenue several times, getting used to her gait and bragging about the mare's speed to several friends. They all noticed Booth was wearing spurs.

After riding, Booth entered Deery's and ordered more drinks. As he sipped a brandy, he stared out the window and observed the passage of a carriage that appeared to contain General Grant and his wife. Booth ran downstairs, untethered his horse, and rode after the vehicle. Riding up to the carriage and peering in, Booth ascertained that it was, indeed, Grant. Booth rode along beside the carriage for a short distance and realized the general was leaving town. This meant, he determined, that Grant's usual military escort would not be present at Ford's Theater that evening.

Around 5:00 P.M. Booth was spotted in Taltavul's bar with James Maddox and Ned Spangler. A few minutes later, he met Atzerodt in the street in front of the bar and spoke with him briefly. Atzerodt had also been drinking heavily and was already quite inebriated. After visiting briefly with the German, Booth, accompanied by Spangler, rode his mare into the alley behind Ford's Theater. He told Spangler to summon Burroughs to hold the reins of his mount while he tended to some business.

Around 5:30 Booth entered Ford's Theater. Twenty minutes later, he was seen leaving the building and entering the National Hotel where he took dinner. During his meal, Booth had several more drinks.

As Booth dined and drank, his fury was building, his hatred for Lincoln raging within. He was overcome with a sense of urgency to reach the president before anyone else. He wanted badly to beat the man who replaced him as leader of the Northern plot, the one Booth perceived as his rival for great and lasting fame.

Chapter V

The Assassination

As late afternoon transitioned into evening on 14 April, an unusual quiet descended on Washington, D.C. As some were later to recall, a perceptible change had taken place in the atmosphere, a darkening, curious, yet mostly unexplainable sensation, the kind that sometimes precedes disaster.

At 7:45 P.M. that night in 1865, the play *Our American Cousin* was scheduled to begin at Ford's Theater. Approximately one-half hour before the curtain was to rise, John Wilkes Booth, now quite drunk, stood in front of the theater with Michael O'Laughlin. Waving his arms and behaving in an agitated manner, Booth exclaimed that the plan had gone awry and that the "major" was not coming, that he refused to go along.

When O'Laughlin asked Booth who the major was, the actor identified him only as the "the major with the president." O'Laughlin still did not understand, and it was apparent to him that Booth was nearly incoherent. To this day, historians remain uncertain as to the identity of the major.

Booth raved on, telling O'Laughlin that his companions wanted to call the whole thing off. Raising his voice, the actor told his friend that he refused to quit now, that the deed must be accomplished this very night.

O'Laughlin finally realized that Booth was talking about assassinating the president. Fearing that his ravings would be overheard by others, he pulled the actor away from the gathering theatergoers and advised him to leave, to forget about the whole thing. Booth angrily refused, telling O'Laughlin it had to be this night or never.

O'Laughlin, still concerned that passersby could overhear their conversation, convinced Booth they should go inside the theater. In a quiet corner of the lobby, they huddled and Booth began making hasty, revised arrangements. Once again, he brought up the "major" and stated that he would wait for his advice. O'Laughlin, finally realizing he could not talk Booth out of his plans, excused himself and left the theater. For several minutes, Booth waited alone in the lobby, glancing at the clock every few seconds. The curtain was about to rise, but President Lincoln and his party had not arrived.

Growing impatient, Booth went outside and rode his mare to the Herndon House. He went directly to Lewis Paine's room where he found the young man waiting. A moment later, Atzerodt arrived and asked where the others were. Booth replied they were apparently not coming, and Atzerodt expressed relief that the mission would have to be cancelled.

Angrily, Booth responded that nothing had been cancelled, that there was only a change of plans because so many things had gone wrong. Too many of the original conspirators had quit, he explained, and there were too many insurmountable difficulties to overcome with regard to kidnapping Vice President Johnson and Secretary of State Seward.

Instead, Booth declared, we will kill them all.

As his two co-conspirators listened, Booth gave instructions to Paine on how Seward should be killed. He then turned to Atzerodt and told him he was to kill Johnson. He, Booth, would slay the president.

Atzerodt, numb with shock, flatly refused, stating he would not kill anyone. Paine considered his new mission for a few seconds and then agreed to participate. Atzerodt left the room.

Moments later, between around 8:30 and 9:00 P.M., Booth mounted his bay mare and rode toward Ford's Theater. According to doorman John Buckingham, Booth entered and departed the theater at least five times between 9:00 and 10:00 P.M. Buckingham also related that the actor appeared highly agitated and was quite drunk.

In spite of several admonitions to refrain from attending the theater, Lincoln was insistent. Several who were originally invited to accompany him, including Stanton, made up excuses not to go.

For a time, Lincoln pondered the wisdom of attending the theater. Earlier in the week, he had related to Lamon the essence of a strange dream he had. In the dream, Lincoln said, he was awakened by sobbing. He rose from his bed and went downstairs to the East Room of the White House where he saw a body dressed in funeral garb and guarded by soldiers. He inquired about the identity of the body from one of the guards and was told it was "The president. He was killed by an assassin!"

Curiously, during the morning of 14 April, residents of Manchester, New Hampshire, were informed that Lincoln had been assassinated!

Another mystery arose from the town of St. Joseph, Minnesota. During most of the afternoon of 14 April, rumors spread throughout the community that the president had been assassinated.

Around 2:30 P.M., a newspaperman in Middletown, New York, received information from an anonymous source that Lincoln had been shot.

Beginning approximately twelve hours before he ever arrived at Ford's Theater, Lincoln's assassination had been reported in at least six newspapers throughout the region.

General and Mrs. Grant were originally invited to attend the play with the president and his wife. The two women did not get along, and the general's wife was determined not to go. Grant offered the excuse that he had made plans to visit his children in New Jersey. Some historians believe General Grant was dissuaded from attending the play by Stanton in the hope that the president would cancel his plans. Other researchers committed to the notion of a conspiracy maintain that Stanton instructed Grant to stay away because he knew what was going to occur that night at Ford's Theater. Still others say that Mrs. Grant simply refused to attend the evening's performance because she despised Mrs. Lincoln. Whatever the case, many have concluded that Grant's presence in the theater box would have encouraged a more efficient security procedure, particularly in the area of the door through which Booth entered.

After being turned down by the Grants, Mrs. Lincoln invited Clara Harris and her fiancé, Major Henry R. Rathbone, to accompany her and the president to the play. Clara was the daughter of New York senator Ira Harris.

The president informed Stanton that he was going to invite Thomas Eckert to accompany him and his wife to the play. Lincoln was impressed with Eckert as a security man and believed he would be quite safe in his presence. Stanton, however, told Lincoln that he had some important work for Eckert to finish and he could not be spared. Ignoring Stanton, Lincoln personally invited Eckert, but the major refused, explaining he had some obligations to Stanton. In essence, both Stanton and Eckert refused Lincoln's request for protective escort.

Lincoln then invited Speaker of the House Schuyler Colfax. Colfax also declined the invitation, claiming he was preparing to leave for the west coast.

Thomas T. Eckert
(Library of Congress photo)

With the play only a few short hours away, Lincoln was making preparations to attend and had no official protection whatsoever!

At 8:15 P.M., President and Mrs. Lincoln left the White House and climbed into the carriage that was to take them to Ford's Theater. As the carriage pulled away, White House door guard Tom Pendel told night guard John Parker to proceed with haste to the theater and be prepared to escort Lincoln and his party to the box.

Subsequent investigation into Parker's role revealed that he had been sponsored by Mrs. Lincoln, who specifically requested he be assigned to the White House.

A few minutes after leaving the White House, the carriage containing the president and the first lady pulled up to the Harris residence and picked up Clara and Major Rathbone. At approximately 8:30 P.M., the carriage arrived at the front of the theater. The four occupants climbed from the coach and, waved on by the doorman John Buckingham, entered the theater. Lincoln carried an overcoat across one arm and his aide carried the president's favorite shawl. Rathbone was dressed in uniform but carried no weapons.

As they walked into the lobby, they were greeted by White House guard John Parker who informed the president he had just come from inspecting the lobby, the stairs, and the presidential box. Since Parker left the White House only a few minutes later than the president, he had hardly been in the theater long enough to conduct a thorough inspection.

As the president and his party entered the theater, the actors on stage paused a moment to acknowledge him and applaud his presence. The orchestra played "Hail to the Chief," and the audience turned to observe the party as it was escorted to the presidential box. Parker held the door to the box open as the four passed through.

Inside the box were a sofa, an armchair, several side chairs, and the black walnut rocking chair preferred by the president.

Once inside, Lincoln stepped up to the railing where he could see and be seen by the audience. He bowed to a standing ovation and thunderous applause. After a moment he mouthed "thank you," and motioned for everyone to be seated. When the last member of the audience was seated, Lincoln backed toward the rocker and sat down. Looking toward the stage, he motioned for the actors to continue.

As Lincoln settled himself into his chair, he was completely unprotected, an uncommon and curious situation for a president of the United States. There were no on-duty guards or policemen at the theater—neither outside in the front and the rear, nor backstage, nor in the audience. The only guard was John Parker, and he would leave his post within minutes. With Parker absent, there was nothing to stop anyone who wished to enter the presidential box.

Lincoln's chair was about four feet away from the door to box seven, and Mrs. Lincoln sat to his immediate right. Miss Harris and Major Rathbone seated themselves on the sofa. Rathbone, by his own estimation, was approximately eight feet from the president. Charles Forbes, Lincoln's footman who arrived in a separate carriage, sat in a straight-backed chair near the door to box eight. It was discovered later that neither of the locks on the doors to the two boxes worked properly.

Directly outside the two doors and just inside the white door though which the party entered, guard John Parker stood next to the chair that had been provided for him. Parker's responsibility was to intercept anyone coming through the white door and prevent them from reaching the president. Parker, however, decided he wanted to watch the play, which could not be seen from his position. He moved his chair through the white door and into the adjacent chamber, but he was still without an adequate view of the performance. Presently, he spotted an empty seat in the gallery and left his post to occupy it, leaving the presidential box completely unguarded.

Historians are in disagreement over whether Parker was merely an inept guard who did not take his duties seriously or part of a plot to leave the president without a guard. The truth will likely never be known. (See Appendix D, The Mystery of John Parker.)

After a few minutes, Parker appeared to grow bored with the performance and returned to stand outside the white door. Presently, he went downstairs into the lobby, paused to look around, and walked outside. He spotted the president's carriage, approached it, and woke the driver Burns. Parker asked Burns if he wanted to go get a drink, and the two men walked toward Taltavul's Star Saloon. On the way, they encountered Lincoln's footman Charles Forbes, who minutes earlier had left his position near the president. Forbes accepted an invitation from the two men to join them and they were soon seated in the bar.

A few moments after Parker, Burns, and Forbes entered Taltavul's, Booth walked through the theater lobby and out into the street where he untied the mare, mounted, and rode into the alley behind the theater. It was approximately 9:30 P.M. Here, he dismounted and shouted for Ned Spangler. When the stagehand did not arrive, he told actor J.L. DeBonay, who was standing nearby, to summon Spangler to hold his horse. Moments later Spangler arrived and informed Booth he was needed to help change scenes. Booth told Spangler to send out John Burroughs. When

Burroughs arrived Booth handed him the reins and entered the theater through the back door.

Booth walked behind the stage set and waved at the actors who remained there awaiting their cues. From where he stood, he looked into the presidential box, but could discern very little.

Booth then entered the dark passageway that led beneath the stage, under the president's box, and into a passageway between the south wall of the theater and Taltavul's Saloon. In the box, Lincoln turned to his wife and told her he had just felt a cold chill. The president turned to ask Forbes for his shawl and discovered the aide was gone, so he rose to put on his overcoat. Lincoln's movement distracted Rathbone, who turned to watch him. When Lincoln sat down, Rathbone noticed the door to box seven was open. He thought little of it and returned his attention to the play.

When Booth exited the passageway, he walked out to Tenth Street, entered the saloon, and spotted Parker, Burns, and Forbes drinking at the bar. Booth walked up to the bar and ordered a whiskey. As he paid for the drink, the actor was approached once again by Ed Henson, who walked out of the gloom from one corner of the saloon and invited Booth to come and join him at his table.

The two men conversed in low tones as they drank, and presently Booth asked Henson if he was still in the mood for some excitement, as he had indicated earlier in the day. Henson said he was. According to Balsiger and Sellier, Booth told Henson to meet him later that night across the Potomac River in Maryland on the road to Upper Marlboro near Good Hope Hill. Henson agreed to do so.

A few minutes later, Booth drunkenly rose from his chair to leave. As he did so, a patron seated at the bar recognized him and said his acting would never equal that of his father's. Incensed at the comment, Booth angrily stalked out of the bar, stating loud enough for all to hear that when he left the stage he would soon be "the most famous man in America."

Moments later, Booth walked up to the doorman at Ford's Theater. He asked Buckingham what time it was, and he was directed to the lobby where a clock hung from the wall. Booth stared at the clock for a moment. It was 10:10 P.M.

It is time, he decided.

While Booth was staring at the clock, George Atzerodt, who decided to disentangle himself from the conspirators, was riding out of town. At about the same time, according to many historians, Lewis Paine, dressed in a heavy, dark coat which concealed a revolver and a large Bowie knife, was riding up to the front door of the home of Secretary of State William Seward in the company of David Herold.

Booth walked behind the dress circle patrons and paused a short distance away from the president's box. He leaned casually against a wall near the door that led to the box and surveyed the theater. He saw the empty chair and thought of Parker drinking at Taltavul's. Actress Jennie Gourlay spotted Booth near the dress circle and noted that he "had a wild look in his eyes."

Quietly and deliberately, Booth moved among the patrons. Acting casually, he looked around the theater. In a moment, he pulled a card from his pocket and handed it to a messenger. The messenger looked at the card, nodded, and led Booth to the white door. The messenger departed immediately, leaving Booth standing alone just outside the door.

Booth paused for a few heartbeats, then pushed open the door and entered into the dim inner corridor. After closing the door behind him, according to writer Roscoe, he "[wedged] it shut with a wooden upright from a music stand," placing it in the cut he had made earlier in the day. Booth then stepped up to the inner door that provided entry into the theater box and placed an eye to the recently bored peephole.

He saw the president seated on the rocking chair watching the play.

As Lincoln and his party were intent on the play, Booth stood just outside in the anteroom. Looking around quickly, he saw no guards anywhere. Deftly, he reached into his coat pocket and withdrew a .44 caliber derringer. The pistol held only one bullet and had earlier been capped and readied for firing. It was approximately 10:15 P.M.

For a few moments, Booth stood just outside the door to the presidential box. His heart raced as the tension, fueled by the alcohol, built inside him.

From the stage, Booth could hear the lines spoken by the mother to her daughter: "Go to your room. You may go to your room at once." As the two women walked off and disappeared stage left, the actor Harry Hawk was then highlighted on center stage. Glancing at the departing pair, he said, "Society, Eh? Well, I guess I know enough to turn you inside out, you sockdologizing old man-trap!"

As the audience responded with laughter, Booth stepped through the door, quickly strode the four feet to the president, and lifted the derringer. As he advanced, Booth reportedly uttered the word, "Freedom."

Lincoln, sensing movement behind him, started to turn his head as Booth pointed the pistol and fired. The ball entered the president's skull about midway between the left

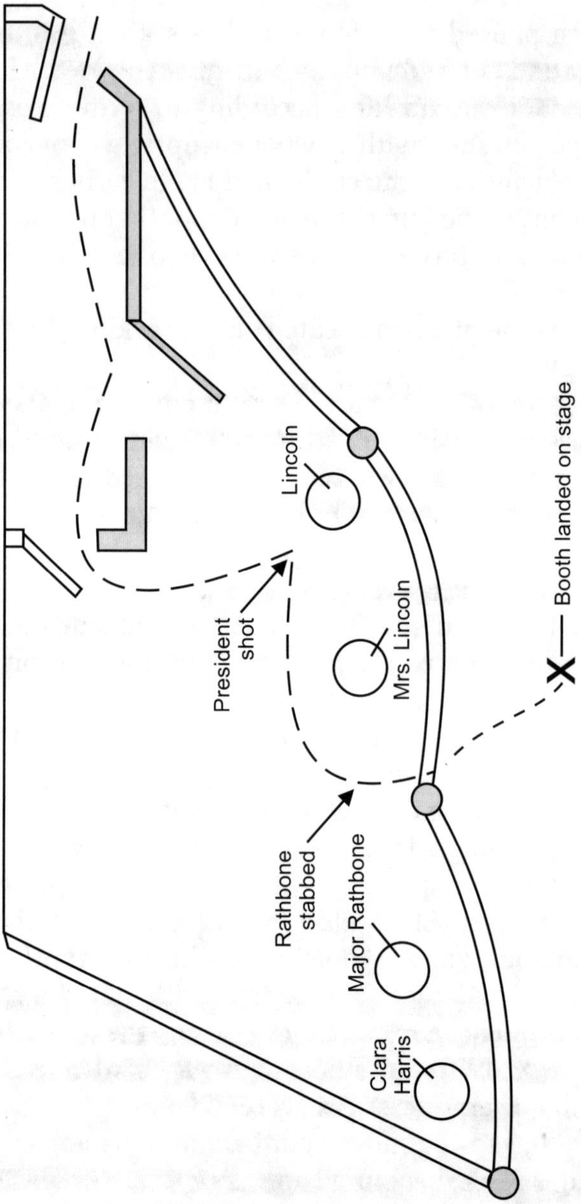

Booth's movements through boxes seven and eight

ear and the median line of the back of the head, inflicting a mortal wound.

Dropping the pistol to the floor and pulling the knife from its belt sheath, Booth cried, “Revenge for the South!”

This one mad act was to forever link the name John Wilkes Booth to assassination. It was also the beginning of one of the greatest controversies and mysteries in American history.

Chapter VI

The Attack On Seward

As the drama within a drama was unfolding at Ford's Theater, a tall, well-built man, believed by many historians to have been Lewis Paine, was riding a one-eyed horse toward the residence of Secretary of State William Seward. Some scholars believe he was guided through the avenues of Washington by David Herold, the young man caught up in the plots and plans of John Wilkes Booth.

On 5 April, Seward, riding in a carriage with his son, daughter, and another person, suffered a serious accident. The team of horses pulling the carriage bolted and the secretary was thrown out, breaking his lower jaw and right arm, as well as tearing ligaments in one foot. As a result, Seward was confined to bed during his recovery.

As the two men rode in the darkness toward Seward's house, located near Lafayette Square, the secretary lay propped up in his bed, his arm in a sling, and his chin secured by a tight leather and steel brace. The apparatus was uncomfortable and it restricted his movements.

Secretary of State
William H. Seward
(Library of Congress photo)

The tall man riding the one-eyed horse was wearing cavalry boots, and around his waist was belted a revolver and a knife. On arriving in front of the secretary's house, he dismounted and, leaving his companion on the street to hold the reins, climbed the few steps to the porch and rang the bell.

Seward's butler, William Bell, opened the door to find a tall, powerfully built man wearing black pants, a long overcoat, and a broad-brimmed hat. He was carrying a bottle in one hand. Once the door was opened, the stranger pushed his way inside and demanded to see Seward. Holding up the bottle and showing it to Bell, he stated he had been sent by Dr. T.S. Verdi with medicine for the secretary.

Bell, maintaining his composure, told the newcomer he was not allowed to see Seward, and he offered to take the medicine to him.

The stranger, brushing past Bell, started climbing the stairs leading to the second floor and Seward's bedroom. At this moment, Frederick Seward, the secretary's son and chief assistant, appeared at the top of the stairs in his nightclothes. Holding up a hand, he signaled for the stranger to stop, telling him he was not allowed up there.

Followed closely by Bell, the stranger reached the top of the stairs and advanced toward Frederick. After two or three steps, he paused, saying he would leave. He turned as if to descend the stairs and then suddenly wheeled around, a navy Colt revolver in his hand. Pointing the weapon at Frederick's chest, the stranger pulled the trigger only to have it misfire. Cursing, he slammed the barrel of the gun across Frederick's head, knocking him to the floor, unconscious. As Frederick lay motionless, the tall stranger struck him again and again.

Witnessing the confrontation, Bell turned, ran down the stairs and out the front door of the residence, screaming, "Murder! Murder!" and hastened to the next door office of General Christopher Augur.

Alarmed by the sudden appearance of Bell, the young man holding the two horses tied his partner's mount to a nearby tree, quickly climbed atop his own, and fled.

The stranger, upset with the malfunctioning revolver, slammed it repeatedly against the banister until the weapon broke. Pulling the large Bowie knife from inside his coat, he proceeded to search along the second floor hallway for Seward's room. Finally locating it, he broke through the door and clumsily stumbled inside where he was met by George Robinson, who was attending the secretary. The intruder lunged at Robinson, slashing a long cut across his forehead. When Robinson fell, the stranger leaped upon Seward, who was lying in the bed, and began stabbing repeatedly at his head. The knife sliced through Seward's right cheek and down the right side of his throat, causing blood to gush out.

As the stranger paused for a moment, Augustus Seward, another of the secretary's sons, ran into the room and attempted to pull him from the bed. Robinson joined Augustus in the effort, and the two succeeded in throwing the assailant to the floor. At the same time, William Seward fell off the other side of the bed.

Awakened by the commotion, Seward's daughter, Fanny, came into the room at this point and was knocked down by the struggling trio. As she watched in horror, the assailant was slashing wildly with the knife and succeeded in plunging it into Robinson's chest and shoulder. One particularly vicious swipe of the blade sliced off a portion of Augustus Seward's scalp.

Suddenly, the stranger rose up and blurted out, "I am mad! I am mad." Still clutching the knife, he turned and bolted from the bedroom. In the hallway, he was met by Bud Hansell, who had just arrived. Hansell, a state department messenger, was stunned into immobility by what he was witnessing and merely watched in confusion as the stranger approached him. The messenger opened his mouth to say something, but before a word was uttered the assailant stabbed the knife deep into his chest.

As Hansell collapsed to the floor, the stranger fled down the stairs and out the front door. Once in the street, the man, now bareheaded and smeared with blood, discovered he had been abandoned by his companion. After untying his horse, he climbed into the saddle and rode at a canter north toward H Street.

As the stranger rode away, William Bell was returning from the Augur house when he spotted him. He pointed at the rider and began screaming that it was the man who had invaded the Seward home. While a few soldiers and passersby were on the street, no one came to his aid. Bell, on foot, pursued the intruder, but ran out of breath after half a block. He watched as the tall man disappeared up Vermont Avenue where he turned east.

Around midnight, a horse was found near the Capitol. It was saddled and bridled and sweating as though someone had recently ridden it very hard. It was somehow determined to be the one ridden by Seward's assailant. Later, it was discovered to be the same one-eyed horse John Wilkes Booth had purchased from a neighbor of Dr. Samuel Mudd. The saddle was subsequently identified as belonging to George Atzerodt, which led to the initial belief that it was the German who tried to assassinate Secretary of State Seward.

On the evening of Monday, 17 April, it was announced by the government that the man who tried to take the life of Seward was Paine.

After abandoning the horse, according to investigators, Paine apparently hid for the next two days in the woods located north of Washington's Fort Lincoln.

As with the assassination of President Lincoln and related events, the attack on Secretary Seward is filled with controversy. Although Lewis Paine was subsequently arrested for the attack, some researchers are convinced that it was actually committed by a man named Lewis Thornton Powell, a name some claim was used by Paine as an alias.

Though researchers Balsiger and Sellier claim to have discovered military records showing that Paine and

Powell were two different men, the U.S. prosecutor, during the Conspiracy Trial, maintained they were the same person. Paine was subsequently convicted and executed. (See Appendix C, The Lewis Paine/Lewis Thornton Powell Controversy.)

Chapter VII

Escape

The sudden sound of Booth's derringer discharging against Abraham Lincoln's head caused Major Rathbone to jerk around. Gun smoke filled a portion of the tiny box, but through the smoke, Rathbone spotted a man standing about seven feet away, his position between the president and the door. As Rathbone gazed in horror, the man dropped a pistol to the floor, shifted a knife from his left hand to his right, and quickly advanced toward the railing.

Rathbone leaped for the assailant, but Booth turned, making a vicious slash at the major and inflicting a severe wound on the biceps of his left arm, a stab that cut clear to the bone.

Booth turned back to the railing and prepared to leap. Rathbone made another lunge at the actor and grasped unsuccessfully at his coat. The nimble actor placed a hand on the railing and vaulted it as he screamed "The South is avenged!" As he plummeted to the stage some twelve feet below, the spur on the heel of his right boot caught on the flag and caused him to land off balance and in a kneeling position, his back toward the audience. On impact, Booth's left tibia snapped two inches above his ankle. As he rose he turned toward the audience and shouted "*Sic Semper Tyrannis!*" "Thus always to tyrants."

The injury notwithstanding, Booth stood up and fled across the stage. He passed close to Henry Hawk, the only actor on stage at the time, and disappeared into the curtains beyond. A blue shred of the flag that hung in front of the president's box had caught on his spur and fluttered from his heel as he ran.

Rathbone, attempting to staunch the flow of blood from his wound, leaned out of the smoke-filled box and yelled, "Stop that man."

Former army officer Joseph B. Stewart was seated in the right front orchestra seat when he was startled by the vaulting man. Stewart immediately recognized Booth as the actor fled across the stage. At Rathbone's cry, Stewart rose from his chair and pursued Booth, also crying, "Stop that man!"

As Booth entered the wings, he almost collided with actress Laura Keene. In the backstage area, he sought the passageway toward the door that opened out into Baptist Alley where John Burroughs still held his horse. In the passageway, he ran into William Withers, the orchestra leader, who made a halfhearted attempt to halt the assassin. Still clutching the knife, the actor slashed at Withers, opening cuts on his neck and side. Booth then fled through the open back door and into the alley.

Subsequent testimony by Mary Jane Anderson, the black woman whose poor domicile faced the alley, revealed that the door was open. She stated that she was "looking through the open door, and noticing the people moving about behind the scenes . . . when all of a sudden I saw Booth burst into the passage . . . and rush to the back door like lightning."

Inside the theater, people were now screaming that the president had been shot.

Stage carpenter Jacob Ritterspaugh was standing in the passageway and made a grab at Booth. The fleeing man raised his knife, and Ritterspaugh, seeing the vicious-looking, blood-smeared weapon, backed away. Ritterspaugh turned to see Spangler standing nearby and stated, "That was Booth!" Spangler told the carpenter to be quiet and not to tell anyone which way he fled.

Stewart was only twenty feet behind Booth as the actor passed through the open back door. Oddly, when Stewart reached the exit it was closed, and he experienced great difficulty opening it.

On entering the dark alley behind the theater, Booth spotted Burroughs tending to the bay mare. Snatching the reins from him, the assassin placed his left foot into the stirrup. Before mounting, he slammed the butt of his knife against the head of Burroughs, knocking him to the ground.

Once in the saddle, Booth had a difficult time controlling the skittish mare. Just as he wheeled the mount and spurred it hard, Stewart finally managed to open the back door and stepped out into the alley just in time to see Booth getting the horse under control. Stewart reached for the reins, but Booth swung the mount around and rode away down the alley.

It is estimated that only a minute passed between the murder of the president and Booth's escape from the theater.

According to author Izola Forrester, Booth's reputed granddaughter, the actor was fleeing through the dark and relatively deserted streets of Washington when he spotted an old friend named Billy Andrews. Booth had known Andrews since childhood. The actor reined up for a moment at recognizing his old chum. Andrews, discerning Booth was in great pain, approached the actor. When Booth quickly explained what had just transpired at Ford's Theater, Andrews pulled a cravat from his neck and bound Booth's broken leg, securing it with a pin. This done, Booth rode on. This seemingly small incident grows in importance in later years.

Back in the presidential box, Rathbone dashed into the antechamber and was surprised to find no guard. When he tried to open the white door, it failed to yield. A length of wood from a music stand about three feet long and four inches wide was wedged between the wall and the door.

From the presidential box, audience members could hear the screaming and wailing of Mary Lincoln. "They've killed him!" she cried over and over. It was now growing clear to the audience what had transpired, and a growing murmur thundered and echoed throughout the theater.

As this was going on, Booth was riding away unimpeded. Though his exact escape route will never be known for certain, it is believed that he rode out of Baptist Alley onto F Street. From there, most believe he turned and galloped his bay hard until reaching Pennsylvania Avenue leading to Capitol Hill. Once on the other side of the Capitol, he headed toward the Navy Yard and the bridge that spanned the Anacostia River.

Meanwhile, several men working together failed to force open the white door to the presidential box. From the inside, Rathbone, despite bleeding profusely from his wound, was finally able to pull away the length of wood holding the door closed. As men tried to force their way into the box, the major blocked their way and shouted for a doctor.

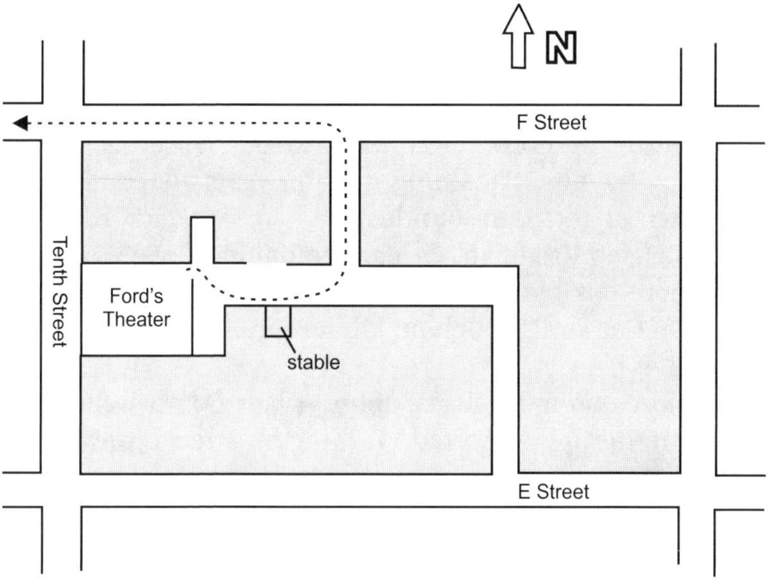

Booth's escape route after leaving Ford's Theater

A young physician named Charles Leale arrived moments later and tended to the wounded president. Leale requested a lamp and ordered the door locked and no one allowed inside save for other physicians. Feeling in the dark with his fingers, Leale found the entry wound at the back of the president's head. There was no exit wound.

Distracted by Rathbone's request for medical help, Leale turned his attention to the major, determined the wound was not serious, and returned to the president. A moment later, Leale rose and announced to all present that the wound was mortal.

Under Leale's direction, the dying president was transported across the street from the theater to the home of William Peterson, 453 Tenth Street. Lincoln was carried into a bedroom and placed on a bed.

By now, theatergoers were rushing from the building shouting that the president had been shot. Inside Ford's Theater, Mrs. Lincoln's screams had turned the place into an "inferno of noise" according to one observer. Other women were also screaming, theater seats were smashed, and cries of terror resounded and created, according to actress Helen Trueman, "a pandemonium that must have been more terrible to hear than that attending the assassination of Caesar. Throughout all the ages it will stand out as the hell of hells."

Almost two miles away, John Wilkes Booth lashed the bay mare through deserted Washington streets toward the Potomac River.

During the seconds following the assassination, Booth was within ten feet of at least a dozen people who knew him well and recognized him immediately. In addition, a number of theatergoers in the audience knew him by sight. Within fifteen minutes following the murder of Lincoln, Booth's name was being shouted by throngs of witnesses. By 11:00 P.M. at least seventeen witnesses had been interviewed by the police, all of whom positively identified Booth as the killer. In spite of all this, the War Department withheld Booth's name from official dispatches and, curiously, would not positively name the assassin until six hours later and would not post his image on a reward notice for six days!

CHAPTER VIII

The Traditional Version of the Flight, the Pursuit, and the Death of John Wilkes Booth

(The perceived movements of John Wilkes Booth and his co-conspirator David Herold from the time of the assassination to the killing at Garrett's barn on 26 April 1865 have been pieced together from the minutes of the trial testimony, from numerous public and military interviews, and from dozens of standard references. The traditionally accepted version of Booth's flight and alleged death at the hands of the authorities is represented as follows.)

— ꕥ —

After guiding the bay mare out of the alley behind Ford's Theater, John Wilkes Booth raced eastward toward the Anacostia River and the Navy Yard Bridge.

At approximately 10:45 P.M., Booth sped down Eleventh Street and approached the bridge, reining in the lathered horse as he neared the sentry station. This end of the bridge was normally closed to travelers after 9:00 P.M. as a wartime precaution, but since the war's end, the order had been rescinded if one had a good reason to pass.

Sergeant Silas T. Cobb confronted the approaching horseman, who was described as hatless, wearing "elegant black boots," a rather pale face, and a "glossy black mustache."

In response to Cobb's question, the rider gave his name as Booth and said he was heading home to Beantown, Maryland. He told Cobb that he had waited this late to travel so that the moonlight would help him find his way. Cobb allowed him to pass.

A few minutes later, a second horseman appeared and Cobb likewise challenged him. The rider gave his name as Smith but Cobb did not believe him. The rider then stated his name was Thomas and said he was heading south to White Plains where he lived. When Cobb asked him why he was traveling so late, the rider said he had been with a woman. Cobb waved him on.

Around 11:00 P.M., John Fletcher, the foreman at Nailor's Livery in Washington rode up to Silas Cobb at the Navy Yard Bridge and asked if a poorly dressed young man riding a roan had passed by recently. Cobb told him one crossed several minutes earlier. Fletcher told him the roan had been stolen and he wanted to pursue the rider. Cobb informed Fletcher that if he crossed over he would not be able to return until in the morning. Without a word, Fletcher turned his mount and rode back into town.

Fletcher rode to the Washington Metropolitan Police station and reported the stolen horse. After explaining his pursuit of the thief to the Navy Yard Bridge, he was taken to the Military Police Headquarters to relate his experience to General C.C. Augur. Fletcher's story, along with those of sixteen other witnesses, convinced Augur and police superintendent A.C. Richards that the killer of the president was John Wilkes Booth and that the assassin, along with David Herold, fled into southern Maryland.

According to the majority of historians, Herold caught up with Booth at Good Hope Hill, about a mile-and-a-half southeast of the Navy Yard Bridge. From there, the pair rode to Surrattsville, Booth's leg causing him severe pain all the way.

Surrattsville was located some eleven miles south of Washington. The Surratt family owned and operated a tavern where the Port Tobacco, Chapel Point, and Leonardtown Roads intersected. Once a popular stagecoach stop, business had dropped off during the war and the place had become neglected and run-down.

Years earlier, Mary Surratt, a widow and Southern sympathizer, had acquired permission to use the tavern as a post office, and her youngest son John was named postmaster. It was believed that the Surrattsville post office eventually became an important letter drop for Confederate agents and was a primary way station on the Confederate underground route that ran from Richmond, Virginia, to Montreal, Canada.

When Booth and Herold arrived at the tavern, they encountered hired innkeeper John Lloyd and instructed him to fetch some supplies that had been stashed in the building earlier by Herold. Lloyd returned with pistols, field glasses, and some tack. Herold had dismounted during the exchange and Booth, who remained on his horse, asked Lloyd for liquor to relieve his pain.

After asking about a doctor, Lloyd told them there was no longer one living in Surrattsville. Booth recalled Dr. Mudd lived just northeast of Bryantown, and the two rode away into the night. Just before the men departed, according to Lloyd's subsequent testimony, Booth exclaimed, "I have murdered the president!"

Around 2:00 A.M. on Saturday morning, 15 April, Booth and Herold rode through the town of TB and left the main route to take a back road toward Bryantown.

Booth and Herold arrived at Mudd's house around 4:30 A.M. Saturday morning. Herold dismounted, walked up onto the porch, and knocked on the door. When Mudd answered, Herold said that his friend, whom he identified as "Mr. Tyson," had been injured in a fall and needed treatment. Mudd came downstairs, opened the door, and admitted the two men, both of whom smelled of whiskey. Booth was apparently taking liquor to ease the pain, and Herold was simply drinking. According to Mudd's later testimony, Herold introduced himself as "Henson."

Mudd later claimed to investigators that the injured man kept his face hidden in a shawl, his chin lowered into it, and acted very suspicious. After placing him on a living room sofa, Mudd cut the boot from his swollen left foot, and on examination, discovered a transverse fracture of the outer bone, the tibia. Mudd set the bone as well as possible under the circumstances and bound it with a splint he fashioned from pieces of a bandbox. Booth was helped up the stairs, led to a second floor bedroom, and placed on a bed. Herold went outside and slept in the barn.

Around noon, Mudd reexamined the injured man's leg. During the examination, Booth kept his face turned, remained silent, and appeared to be suffering not only from pain but also from fatigue. Mudd had his hired man make a pair of homemade crutches for his injured guest, and he let the visitor sleep throughout the remainder of the afternoon. Booth paid Mudd twenty-five dollars for his service.

Sometime later, Herold asked Mudd for directions to the home of Colonel Samuel Cox's Wicomico-Potomac plantation, a location that, like Surratt's tavern, often served the Confederate underground. Late in the afternoon, Dr. Mudd left his house on an errand. A short time afterward, Booth and Herold mounted up and rode away into Zekiah Swamp, which extended southward from Mudd's house.

Following a trail that wound through the swamp, Booth and Herold became lost several times, finally arriving at Cox's farm around midnight. At Cox's they asked about a boat to take them across the Potomac River and were told that none was available, and that Union soldiers were patrolling the roads and the river.

Booth and Herold were led to a hiding place in the woods by Cox's foster brother, Thomas A. Jones, another Rebel sympathizer. Each evening for the next six nights, Jones carried food, liquor, and newspapers to the fugitives.

During this time of hiding out in the woods near Cox's farm, Booth suffered terribly from the pain in his leg. It rained often, and the temperature dropped, making the environment somewhat uncomfortable. Jones continued to bring him brandy to help ease his suffering.

On 20 April, Stanton issued a proclamation offering a total of $100,000 in reward money. The capture of the president's assassin would bring $50,000. Reward money in the amount of $25,000 each was offered for John H. Surratt and David C. Herold who were listed as Booth's accomplices.

The proclamation also stated that "all persons harboring or secreting [the fugitives], or aiding or assisting in their concealment and escape . . . will be treated as accomplices in the murder of the president and the attempted assassination of the secretary of state, and shall be subject to trial before a military commission and the punishment of death."

On Friday, 21 April, Jones persuaded a fisherman named Henry Rowland to secrete a rowboat into a Potomac River backwater near Dent's Meadow. That evening, Jones led Booth and Herold to the boat and helped the injured actor into the stern. After handing Jones some money and a bottle of whiskey, Herold rowed away.

It is believed by most researchers that Herold rowed upstream to Nanjemoy Creek just west of the Port Tobacco River. Some scholars are convinced he traveled in this direction in search of a Confederate blockade-runner. Whatever the case, no such boat was available. As the two men hid in Nanjemoy Cove all the next day, Union boats patrolled the Potomac channel while troops searched the banks. At sundown, Herold rowed out of the cove toward Mathias Point on the Virginia side of the river.

Early Sunday morning, 23 April, Herold landed the boat at Mathias Point. Booth and Herold walked a short distance to the home of a Mrs. Quesenberry. Following a short visit, the woman directed the two men to the residence of Dr. Richard Stewart, yet another Confederate sympathizer. By this time, Stewart had learned of the assassination of the president, the search for the fugitives, and the threat to hang anyone aiding them. Nervously, he provided a meal for Booth and Herold and then sent the two men to stay at the poor cabin of his black slave, William Lucas.

Early Monday morning, Lucas transported Booth and Herold southwest to Port Conway on the Rappahannock River in a spring wagon. Herold handed the black man ten dollars for his help and sent him away. After climbing out of the wagon, Herold spotted three Confederate cavalrymen and requested an escort some distance to the south. The riders agreed to accompany the fugitives to the home of Richard Garrett a few miles away. Garrett had a reputation for helping Southerners in need. A short time later, a ferry arrived and carried the two fugitives and the three troopers across the river to Port Royal on the opposite shore.

At the Garrett farm, Booth was introduced as "John W. Boyd," a Confederate soldier whose leg was wounded at Richmond. Booth remained at the farm while Herold rode into Bowling Green with the cavalrymen.

On Tuesday morning, Herold returned to the Garrett farm, and he and Booth spent most of the day sitting on the front porch resting and visiting with Garrett's sons. Around sundown, horsemen dressed in Confederate gray rode up to the porch and announced that Union soldiers were spotted crossing the Rappahannock River and were heading toward their location.

At Port Conway, a twenty-five-man cavalry detail led by Luther Baker, Lt. Edward P. Doherty, and Lt. Colonel Conger learned from ferryman William Rollins that a crippled man hobbling on crutches and accompanied by a younger man had crossed the river to Port Royal. Once in Port Royal, Baker learned that a Confederate trooper named Willie Jett had led the men down the road toward Bowling Green.

About an hour later, Booth and Herold spotted a squadron of Federal cavalry approaching along the road to Bowling Green. They left Garrett's front porch and fled into the woods behind the tobacco barn. One of Garrett's sons watched as the two fled, and their hasty departure caused him to grow suspicious.

Concerned that the Federals were seeking the guests, Garrett's oldest son approached the men in the woods and suggested they be on their way in the morning so as not to create any problems for his father.

Later that evening when the two came out of hiding, the injured man told the oldest son he didn't want to sleep in the house. The strangers were led to the tobacco barn and told they were welcome to spend the night there. Convinced the two men were fugitives and concerned they might try to steal some of the horses on leaving, the son locked them in the barn.

In Bowling Green, Baker located Jett at the home of his fiancée. The Rebel was immediately taken prisoner and questioned at the point of a gun.

On learning that Jett's passengers had stopped at Garrett's farm, Baker, Conger, Dougherty, and the troop, along with Willie Jett, raced back up the road. Around 3:00 A.M., the contingent arrived at a position approximately one hundred yards southwest of Garrett's house. After dismounting and tying the horses, the troopers crept up to the structure. Conger reminded the troops that Booth was to be taken alive, and Baker deployed them around the house. Baker and Dougherty then went to the front door and knocked loudly. When Garrett opened the door, he was immediately grabbed by Baker, pulled outside, and questioned.

Baker asked Garrett where he was hiding Booth. The farmer only replied that a man named Boyd had stopped the previous day but fled into the woods with his companion when the Union soldiers were spotted.

Baker and Conger were convinced Garrett was lying, so they pulled him into the yard and threatened to hang him from a nearby locust tree unless he told them the truth.

At this point, Garrett's sons, who had been keeping watch over the horses, arrived. As soon as the oldest discerned the reason for the appearance of the soldiers, he told Conger that the men he was looking for were sleeping in the tobacco barn.

Once the location of the barn was pointed out, Dougherty ordered several troopers to surround it. Baker and Conger walked up to the closed door of the structure and hailed the men inside, ordering them to lay down their weapons and come out.

For the next twenty minutes, Baker and Conger conversed with Booth, who remained in the barn. The two officers urged the fugitive to surrender, but Booth refused to give up, offering instead to fight it out man to man.

Finally, Conger told Booth to surrender or the barn would be set afire. At this point, Herold began to cry out, stating he wanted to give himself up. Herold's admission drew curses and recriminations from Booth.

As Booth berated the young man, Herold walked toward the door, which was now unlocked and opened slightly. Baker told Herold to extend his arms through the open door, and as soon as he did, the lieutenant grabbed his wrists and pulled him roughly outside. Several cavalrymen seized Herold, dragged him some distance away, and tied him to a tree. Herold cried and whimpered, begging for mercy and claiming he had no role in the assassination of the president of the United States.

Baker and Dougherty continued their dialog with the man inside the barn. As they did so, Conger walked around to the rear of the building, struck a match to a wad of straw or corn husks, and thrust the burning mass though a gap in the planks.

Almost immediately, a great blaze took hold of the dry material inside the barn. Flames illuminated the interior, and the men standing outside could look through the gaps and see a figure standing inside, a man propped up on a crutch and facing the door, a rifle held close to his chest.

As the troopers watched in fascination, the figure suddenly dropped the rifle, picked up a small table, and turned to strike at the approaching flames. Seeing that this effort was useless in stopping the blaze, the figure threw the table to the ground and turned back toward the front door, drawing a pistol from his belt as he did so. Suddenly, a shot was heard above the din of the inferno, and the man in the burning barn pitched forward, falling face down onto the ground.

Reacting quickly, Baker leaped into the open doorway, snatched the revolver from the dying man's hand, and pulled the spasming body outside. After dragging it several feet from the burning barn, Baker was approached by Conger, who asked the lieutenant why he had shot the fugitive. Stunned, Baker looked up at his fellow officer and told him he thought he, Conger, had shot him. Dougherty joined the two men and asked if Booth had committed suicide.

Confusion as to who shot the man reigned for several minutes until a trooper, Sergeant Boston Corbett, came forward and admitted firing the shot, stating that God had told him to do so. Other troopers standing nearby laughed and jeered when they heard this admission, no one believing this former insane asylum inmate could or would do such a thing.

Meanwhile, the dying man was carried to Garrett's front porch and laid down gently on the boards. He had been struck by a pistol ball in the nape of the neck, the shot severing the spinal column. The man was in intense pain and begged for water, his voice a mere whispering gasp. Baker sent one of the troopers to fetch a doctor.

A short time later, Dr. Urquhart arrived from Port Royal and attempted to get the dying man to drink, but he was not able to swallow. Urquhart told Baker the man would not live much longer.

Minutes later, the man on the front porch looked around at the faces hovering over him and begged them to kill him, but no one moved. The barn collapsed and Garrett's roosters started to crow.

Finally, around 7:00 A.M. Wednesday, 26 April, the man died. It was announced later that day that John Wilkes Booth, assassin of President Abraham Lincoln, had met his fate.

CHAPTER IX

Manhunt

(Continuous and intensive investigation into the traditional version of the flight and alleged death of John Wilkes Booth has yielded a number of pertinent and troubling inconsistencies. Furthermore, with the passage of time, additional information has been discovered that casts doubt on many aspects of the accepted history. Following a critical analysis of the traditional materials and utilizing information only recently made available, a revised sequence of events is presented in the next five chapters, events that, in many cases, contradict the established accounts regarding the pursuit and fate of John Wilkes Booth.)

Moments after killing the president of the United States, John Wilkes Booth whipped his tired mare beyond the outskirts of Washington and toward the Navy Yard Bridge. The Navy Yard was located near the end of Eighth Street. The bridge, a wooden structure, spanned the Anacostia River (sometimes referred to as the Eastern Branch), a tributary of the Potomac River.

Around 10:30 P.M., Booth rode up to the small guardhouse positioned at the Washington end of the bridge. As he approached, a sentry stepped out to greet him. The sentry, Sergeant of the Guard Silas T. Cobb, had been given orders to deny passage of anyone across the bridge after 9:00 P.M. unless they had written permission from some authority.

Cobb asked the hatless rider to identify himself, and Booth provided his name. When Cobb asked Booth where he was going, the actor replied he was on his way home to Charles. Charles was the county immediately south and west of Prince Georges County. Booth told Cobb he lived near Beantown.

The Navy Yard Bridge
(Library of Congress photo)

Cobb informed Booth that no one was allowed to pass after 9:00 P.M. According to chronicler Benn Pitman, Booth told Cobb he was unaware of the restriction and said, "I had business in the city and thought if I waited I'd have the moon to ride home by."

The sergeant, believing the rider to be an innocent reveler in Washington who merely lost track of the time, stepped aside to let him pass. Booth rode across the bridge and a short time later crossed the border into Maryland.

During his testimony at the subsequent trial of the conspirators, Cobb stated Booth was riding a small bay. The horse had been ridden hard, and both mount and rider seemed uneasy.

Curiously, fifteen minutes following the shooting of President Lincoln, all of the telegraph wires in the city of Washington were severed! Scholars are convinced that the only person who knew enough about the telegraph system to render it inoperable was Major Thomas Eckert. When Eckert was informed of this catastrophe, he stated he was too busy to look into it. Sabotage was immediately suspected, but investigations into the matter were never forthcoming.

Less than ten minutes after Booth crossed the Navy Yard Bridge, Sergeant Cobb stopped a second rider approaching the bridge and asked his name. The newcomer identified himself as "Smith" and told the guard he was heading to his home in White Plains. When Cobb indicated he did not believe Smith was his real name, the rider immediately changed it to "Thomas." When Cobb asked him why he was out so late, "Thomas," who was riding a roan, replied he had been in bad company. Cobb invited the rider to come closer, and after examining him and his roan in the lamplight emanating from the guardhouse door, he waved him on.

Most historians have written that this second rider was David Herold. Recently uncovered information, along with Cobb's own testimony, cast serious doubt on this identification. Furthermore, provocative discoveries by researchers Balsiger and Sellier provide evidence suggesting the rider was actually Ed Henson.

During Cobb's subsequent testimony at the trial of the conspirators, the prosecution ordered David Herold to stand up. Cobb stated that Herold was "very near the size of the second horseman; but, I should think, taller, although I cannot be sure, as he was on horseback." Cobb also stated, under oath, that the man who crossed the bridge that night had a "lighter complexion" than Herold. In short, Cobb was not at all certain who crossed the Navy Yard Bridge after Booth.

Within a few minutes after "Smith" crossed the bridge, a third rider arrived, pulling his mount right up to Cobb. Before the guard could say anything, the rider identified himself as John Fletcher, an employee of Nailor's Livery Stable. He said he was chasing a stolen horse, a roan. Cobb decided the newcomer "did not seem to have any business on the other side of the bridge," so he turned him away. Fletcher reined his mount around and rode back to the city.

As Fletcher rode back into town, he was relatively certain that the man who entered the stable in the dark and stole the horse was David Herold, who had visited Nailor's establishment several times during the previous week. Fletcher rode back to the stable and was putting away his horse when he learned from passersby that the president had been shot. Fletcher walked out to Fourteenth Street, encountered a cavalry sergeant, and asked him if any stray horses had been rounded up. The sergeant replied in the affirmative and suggested Fletcher proceed to Metropolitan Police headquarters on Tenth Street to inquire. Fletcher did so and, while he was there, reported the theft of the roan and provided a name and description of the man he believed stole the animal.

Thus, it is only on Fletcher's say-so that most of the world believes it was David Herold who crossed the Navy Yard Bridge minutes after Booth.

According to materials examined by Balsiger and Sellier, Henson rode to Good Hope Hill, located approximately one-and-a-half miles southeast from the bridge. On approaching the summit of the low prominence, he heard his name called. Bringing his horse to a halt, he looked around, spotted Booth, and returned the greeting.

Booth, still breathing heavily from his ride and grimacing from the pain in his broken leg, told Henson he had killed the president and asked his companion if he was throwing in with him. Henson said he was. Booth told him how he had broken his leg during the leap from the theater box to the stage, stating that it was beginning to hurt badly.

The plan, according to Booth, was to ride toward Upper Marlboro, some ten miles to the east. After stopping there, he explained to Henson, they would turn south and ride some twenty miles to Benedict's Landing on the Patuxent River. There, they would board a ship registered to England but flying a Canadian flag.

But first, Booth said, they needed to stop at the tavern in the old Surratt house at Surrattsville, some seven miles to the southeast.

As Booth and Henson rode toward Surrattsville, Secretary of War Stanton ordered all routes out of Washington closed. Curiously, all exits were covered save for the Navy Yard Bridge, the most logical route for the assassin to take. Documents in the War Department archives prove conclusively that it was well known at the time that this route was part of the so-called Underground Railway traveled by Confederate messengers, smugglers, and spies. A search of War Department files, however, has failed to yield any information whatsoever that this avenue of escape was even considered by Stanton.

According to historians, Secretary of War Stanton knew a great deal about Booth and his planned escape route, but his decisions relative to pursuit apparently took none of this information into consideration. Many conspiracy theorists claim Stanton wanted Booth to get away. Others maintain Stanton wanted to confuse and divert federal and police patrols so that his own men had time and opportunity to capture and kill Booth.

On the way to Surrattsville, Booth told Henson that some arms, ammunition, and other things they needed were stored inside the tavern. They arrived around midnight, and while Booth remained on his horse, Henson dismounted and knocked on the tavern door, waking a drunk John Lloyd, the proprietor.

Following a short discussion with Lloyd, Henson went inside and returned a few minutes later with a drink for Booth, along with a carbine and a package containing several items. He also carried two bottles of brandy. Booth asked Henson to inquire about a doctor, but Lloyd said there wasn't one nearby anymore. The closest, he said, was Dr. Mudd who lived three-and-a-half miles north of Bryantown and near the head of Zekiah Swamp. As the two rode off, Lloyd later testified, he heard them talking about having killed the president.

Around 2:00 A.M., and after riding three-and-a-half miles, Booth and Henson passed through the small community of TB, continued along the road to where it crossed the Mattawoman Swamp, three miles farther south, and then onto the road that led past St. Peter's Church and to the home of Dr. Samuel Mudd.

By the time Booth and Henson were on their way to Dr. Mudd's house, Stanton's press releases relative to the pursuit of the president's assassin did not even mention Booth's name, even though the killer was already known to dozens of people. It was not until 4:45 A.M. on Saturday morning, 15 April, that Booth was formally identified by Stanton as the murderer, and even then the information was kept quiet.

Most Lincoln-era historians agree that if Stanton wanted Booth captured, he would have made certain the actor's name was broadcast far and wide as soon as his role in the assassination was determined. Stanton, however, was apparently in no hurry to capture Booth or to inform the country of the identity of the murderer. The War Department effectively withheld the assassin's name until the afternoon papers of the following day were already out.

Cavalry troops were already patrolling roads paralleling the Potomac River, roads leading to Barnesville, Darnestown, and Tenlytown. Soldiers had orders to intercept all vessels on the Potomac from Washington to Point Lookout where the river joined the Chesapeake Bay. Stanton also had all roads leading to Virginia blocked, but by the time the order was carried out, Booth had ridden fifty miles. By Easter Sunday morning, the mouth of the Patuxent River was closed, and the entire western shore of the Chesapeake Bay east of the capital was thick with army and navy patrols.

Booth managed to evade the roadblocks for several reasons: He had a good head start; the blockings were haphazardly undertaken; the earliest roadblocks had been established in the least likely direction Booth would have taken.

Furthermore, the only road Stanton had not closed was the one that ran from Washington to Port Tobacco, precisely the one taken by Booth. Even stranger, it was learned later that Stanton had actually been told by Louis Weichmann that the Port Tobacco road was the one Booth had planned on using.

When Captain James William Boyd heard the news of the Lincoln assassination, he was stunned, disappointed, and frightened. Booth, he realized, had completely destroyed his plan to kidnap the president. Boyd was now concerned that the subsequent investigation into the assassination would eventually lead to him and that he would be in great danger. The Confederate spy was convinced he would be set up to take the blame and would receive no protection whatsoever from the Union speculators or from Stanton, the man who initially enlisted his services. He also feared that, once captured, he would be tried for the killing of Thomas Watkins.

Boyd decided the only thing for him to do was to run. Hurriedly, he packed a small bag and rode into Maryland.

Superintendent of Washington's Metropolitan Police force Major A.C. Richards reviewed liveryman John Fletcher's description of the events involving the stolen horse. Richards, in fact, had been enjoying the play at Ford's Theater at the time of the assassination and had just returned to his office. Acting on his own initiative, Richards deduced the sequence of events from the theater to the Navy Yard

Bridge. He wanted to send out a posse of policemen immediately in pursuit of the assassin, but, as researcher Roscoe has explained, law enforcement protocol limited his authority in this matter and kept him "chained to his desk."

Richards ordered Detective John Clarvoe to summon twelve policemen and go in pursuit of the suspected assassins. Richards was confronted with a major problem—the Metropolitan Police did not have any horses. The military, on the other hand, had hundreds of available mounts, so he requested some from them. At first, the military did not want to provide horses to Richards. It is believed that members of the military were more concerned about earning rewards than in actually assisting Richards in the capture of Booth. Finally, after laboring through a dense network of government red tape, Richards was finally able to obtain enough horses for his policemen. By the time the horses were delivered and ready to go, however, the escapees had a ten-hour head start.

Booth's fractured leg was causing him great pain as he and Henson neared the home of Dr. Samuel Mudd. Though Mudd's residence was well off the route to the rendezvous on the Patuxent River, Booth determined it was necessary. In addition, he said, there was yet a second British ship anchored at Port Tobacco, located about a dozen miles southwest of Mudd's farm. Booth told Henson the ship would take them out of the bay, into the Atlantic Ocean, and thence on to England.

At approximately four o'clock Saturday morning, Booth and Henson rode into the yard in front of Dr. Mudd's home. Prior to arriving, Booth donned false whiskers in the hope Mudd would not recognize him.

As the two men guided their mounts toward the house, they spotted Mudd watching them from his second floor bedroom window. Henson dismounted and called out that his friend had a broken leg and needed attention.

When Mudd opened the front door, Henson introduced himself and, nodding toward Booth, said his name was Tyler. "Tyler," Mudd related later, had a heavy beard and kept a shawl wrapped around the lower part of his face. With help from Henson, Mudd helped Tyler off his horse.

Mudd invited the men into the house and led Tyler to a bed in the front room. The left ankle was swollen badly, forcing the doctor to cut away the leather boot. After examining the leg, Mudd discerned "a slight fracture of the tibia about two inches above the ankle," Mudd told Tyler it was not a particularly dangerous injury. While Tyler complained of back pains, Mudd splinted the leg with pieces of a bandbox and bandaged it. With help from Henson, he carried the injured man to the second floor and placed him in a bed to rest. Mudd also provided him with an old shoe for the left foot.

Around 7:00 A.M., about two hours after treating Tyler, Mudd sat down to breakfast with Henson and engaged in small talk during the meal. A tray of food was sent upstairs to Tyler.

At 7:22 A.M., 15 April, President Abraham Lincoln died from the wound inflicted by John Wilkes Booth. Surgeon-General Dr. Ezra W. Abbott folded Lincoln's arms over his chest. The Reverend Phineas Gurley, who was standing nearby, whispered "Our Father and our God," and began to pray. Following the prayer, Stanton is reputed to have said, "Now he belongs to the ages."

Around eight o'clock. Saturday morning, police superintendent Richards dispatched a posse to Surrattsville. On arriving, the policemen banged on the door of the tavern, awakening John Lloyd. When he came out, they asked him if he knew anything about the whereabouts of Booth and Herold, and he replied that he did not. Lloyd then sent the policemen away on a false lead.

Ford's Theater on the day after the assassination with black mourning ribbons draped across the building. (Library of Congress photo)

Under orders from Stanton, Lt. David D. Dana, brother to Assistant Secretary of War Charles A. Dana, was busily establishing a command post at Piscataway, less than ten miles northwest of Dr. Mudd's house. From Piscataway, Dana wired Assistant Adjutant-General Chandler that he had arrived and had posted his troops, thus making it "impossible for [the fugitives] to get across the river in this direction." Strangely, in the same message, Dana told Chandler he had "reliable information that the person who murdered Secretary Seward" was a man named Boyd, "the man who killed Captain Watkins in Maryland."

While in Piscataway, Dana sent a message to a small command at Chapel Point near Port Tobacco. He informed them that the president had been assassinated and directed them to scatter out along the shores of the Patuxent River to the east. This order was rather odd in that instead of leaving the troops right on the route Booth was presumed to travel, a well-known and oft-used Confederate route, he dispersed them to a region where there was no chance at all of finding the fugitive. Historians have long pondered this strange and illogical order. No one knows if it was at the initiative of Lt. Dana or if it came directly from Stanton. Whatever the case, Dana's patrol, according to Roscoe, was "hobbled."

In New York, NDP chief Colonel Lafayette C. Baker received a telegram from Stanton requesting he come to Washington and assist in finding the president's assassin. Only five days earlier Stanton had accused Baker of conspiring to do the same thing. When Baker arrived, Stanton told him, "They have now performed what they have long threatened to do. You must go to work."

According to author Dewitt, Baker quickly determined the aim of Booth had been to cross the Potomac and land on the Virginia shore as close as possible to the Rappahannock, cross it, and then turn west and flee into the mountains of Kentucky or Tennessee. Virtually all of Virginia was placed under military control.

The trail was growing cold, however, and men in the field seemed somehow reluctant to share with Baker all they learned about the fugitives. During his career, Baker had stepped on many toes and was not a popular officer among the soldiers.

Following breakfast, Henson asked Dr. Mudd for directions; he wanted to know the quickest route for reaching the Potomac River. Mudd pointed toward Zekiah Swamp, just beyond the boundary of his farm. Though the shortest route, he said, the swamp contained quicksand and was sometimes a hazardous journey. On the south side of the swamp, he explained, was the Wicomico River, a tributary of the Potomac.

After listening intently to the directions, Henson asked Mudd if he could borrow a razor so Tyler could shave. While Mudd rummaged thorough a drawer for a razor, Henson inquired about the possibilities of renting a carriage for a couple of days. Mudd said he needed to ride into Bryantown later and would look into the matter.

A group of Metropolitan policemen, as well as some National Detective police led by Major James R. O'Bierne, entered Booth's room at the National Hotel on two separate occasions, a room registered in the name of George Atzerodt. From the two searches, authorities found a Colt revolver, a Bowie knife, a handkerchief monogrammed "Mary R.E. Booth," a pair of slippers, a pair of trousers, and a half-empty bottle of hair oil. They also found Booth's trunk, which contained a Confederate colonel's uniform, several photographs, a map, a letter from someone named Jenny in Canada, and a number of clues relative to the kidnap and assassination plots along with mention of several of Booth's accomplices. One item was a letter written by Samuel Arnold in which he mentioned a kidnap plot. Another item was an iron-handled gimlet that was believed to have been the implement used to bore the hole in the door of box seven at Ford's Theater.

According to Balsiger and Sellier, Washington blacksmith James Booth (no relation to John Wilkes) was a neighbor to the Herold family on Eighth Street. On the afternoon of Good Friday, 14 April, Booth's sixteen-year-old son, Johnny, left with David Herold for a horseback ride into Maryland. Herold had an opportunity to sell a horse and made an appointment with the prospective buyer. When the pair had not returned by Friday evening, the blacksmith grew concerned and decided to go looking for them. He hitched up a buggy and rode down the road that wound past Dr. Mudd's house into Bryantown. On several occasions, the blacksmith was forced to pull his buggy to the side of the road to allow the passage of soldiers and cavalry.

It wasn't until early Saturday morning that he finally found his son at the home of Walter Edeline. The youth and Herold had gotten drunk and fallen asleep on Edeline's front porch. The father woke his son, helped him into the buggy, and returned to Washington. David Herold was left sleeping on the porch.

Around mid-afternoon on Saturday, Henson received word from Mudd that no carriages were available. They had all been rented by area farmers to transport their families to Easter services the following day. Mudd remained in Bryantown to conduct some business.

Mrs. Mudd determined Tyler would not be able to walk without crutches. Since there were none in the house, she asked her gardener to fashion a pair from available materials. Henson took the crutches upstairs to Tyler, and about an hour later he was helping him negotiate the stairway down to the first floor.

As the two descended the stairs, Mrs. Mudd noticed that Tyler had shaved off his moustache, and that his whiskers, clearly a false beard, "had become detached."

Henson informed Mrs. Mudd they would be leaving shortly. Noting that Tyler was in great pain, she cautioned them not to travel. Before another hour passed, however, the two men climbed onto their horses and rode away into the swamp. It was between 4:00 and 5:00 P.M. A short time later, Dr. Mudd returned from Bryantown with the news that the president had been assassinated. He told his wife that the roads were crowded with military patrols.

Later that evening, Mrs. Mudd told her husband about the fake beard worn by the man named Tyler. She suggested there was something quite suspicious about the two visitors and encouraged her husband to ride back to Bryantown to report the incident.

Booth and Henson rode along a cart road that wound through the upper section of Zekiah Swamp. This swamp, approximately fifteen miles long and one mile wide, wound in a southwesterly direction from near Mudd's house to Allen's Fresh, a small settlement where the Wicomico River broadens into a wide backwater of the Potomac River. Squatters and woodcutters lived in isolated locations throughout much of the lower part of the swamp, mostly along Allen's Creek. Trappers occasionally entered the area in search of raccoon, muskrat, and opossum. The dense foliage blotted out most of the sunlight, and deep pools of dark water often forced travelers to leave the dim trail and hack their way through the undergrowth.

Presently, the two riders came upon a crude residence. A short distance from the ramshackle cabin and in the inky darkness of the thick woods stood a black man who quietly watched the newcomers approach. The two rode toward him and asked for directions to the farm of Samuel Cox. The black man, Oswald Swann, remained in the shadows but pointed down the trail and provided directions.

Having difficulty understanding him, the strangers told Swann to get a horse and lead them to the Cox farm. Swann climbed aboard a swaybacked mare and rode up to the two men. Looking them over, he noticed one was carrying crutches. Swann indicated the direction they were to travel and, placing his horse in the lead, rode down the path. The strangers followed single file.

Sometime between midnight and 4:00 A.M. Easter Sunday, the three men arrived at Rich Hill, the name of the Cox farm. Samuel Cox, the owner, heard the approaching riders and came out to greet them. Several minutes passed in conversation between the two white men while Swann stood some distance away.

Cox, like many landowners in this part of Maryland, was a Southern sympathizer and known to offer help to Confederates from time to time. By way of identification, Booth showed Cox the initials on his hand. It appeared to Swann that Cox then provided directions, and the two strangers rode away in the company of Cox's overseer, Franklin Robey. After Cox reentered his house, Swann turned his horse and rode back to his home in the swamp.

Early the following morning, Cox rode down the path taken by the two strangers. After traveling about one-half mile, he encountered them lying in a ditch. The man who identified himself as John Wilkes Booth was obviously in great pain as a result of his broken leg.

With help from Cox and Henson, Booth was placed on his horse, and the trio rode another mile toward the south until reaching a dense, nearly impenetrable pine thicket located not far from a tributary of the Potomac River.

On returning to his farm later that morning, Cox sent word to his foster brother Thomas A. Jones that he needed to see him immediately. Jones was originally from Port Tobacco and owned a small farm about four miles south and slightly west of Cox's. Jones was also a well-known Southern sympathizer, had once been arrested and detained in a federal prison, despised Lincoln, and during the war often transported people and goods across the Potomac River into Virginia in his boat.

When Jones arrived at Cox's farm at nine o'clock, he was told by his foster brother that Lincoln's assassin and a companion were hiding in the swamp and that they needed transportation across the river.

Jones said such a trip would be risky with all of the military on the lookout for Booth. He told Cox he needed to talk to the two men. Cox gave him directions to the pine thicket, about two miles west of the house, and instructed Jones to carry food and drink to the men.

The pine thicket in which Booth and Henson lay in hiding was dark, cold, and uncomfortable. From this location, the two fugitives could occasionally hear the passage of cavalry along the road some distance away. They were to remain here for six days and five nights.

When Jones was about fifty yards away from the thicket, he spotted Booth's bay mare, still saddled and bridled, grazing in a tiny clearing. Jones caught the horse and tied it to a tree.

As he approached the hiding place, Jones gave a whistle, a signal previously agreed upon by Cox and Booth. Presently, Henson stepped from behind cover, pointing a carbine at the newcomer. Jones identified himself, showed Henson the food and drink, and was taken to Booth. The actor was lying on the ground and partially covered by a blanket. Lying next to him were a rifle, two pistols, a knife, and his crutches.

In his book *John Wilkes Booth: An Account of His Sojourn in Southern Maryland after the Assassination of Abraham Lincoln, his Passage Across the Potomac, and his Death in Virginia*, published in 1893, Jones relates that Booth was dressed in travel-stained black clothes, but otherwise his appearance was "respectable." He stated Booth "wore a mustache and his beard had been trimmed about two or three days before."

Jones, realizing Booth was in intense pain, told him he would take him across the river as soon as the patrols thinned out somewhat. To do it now, he explained, would be foolhardy. He told the two men he would bring them food and liquor every day until such time as they could cross.

During his visit, Jones stated that he had seen the bay horse grazing nearby. He suggested the presence of the animal might betray their hiding place. Some time later, according to Balsiger and Sellier, Henson moved the horses some distance from the thicket and shot them. It is believed the animals were led into quicksand before being shot, for they were never found.

When Jones reached his home that evening, he summoned Henry Woodland (sometimes identified as Rowland), a free black and his employee. He told Woodland to go fishing every morning in the boat that was kept at Dent's Meadow on the Potomac. If any federal officers were watching, explained Jones, they would be convinced that was what the boat was for.

At church on Easter Sunday, 16 April, Mudd told his brother George about the visit from the two men. He stated he provided medical assistance to one of them and admitted he was rather suspicious of the pair. Later in the day, George related this information to Lt. Alexander Lovett. The two men then rode to Samuel Mudd's house where the officer questioned the physician. Mudd told Lovett he never got a good look at the injured man's face, and that his guest complained often of pain in his back, likely brought on by spending a long time on horseback. Every time he approached the patient, said Mudd, he would cover his head with his shawl. Mudd told Lovett that he hastily fashioned a crude splint, and that the injured man said something about hurrying on so that a family physician could examine the break.

By the time he was finished questioning Dr. Mudd, Lovett was convinced the injured man was John Wilkes Booth and said so. Appearing startled, Mudd admitted he had met Booth months earlier, but he insisted that the man who stopped at his house could not have been the actor.

Once finished with his questions, Alexander Lovett bade the Mudds good-bye and rode away. Only after the officer was gone did Mudd recall the boot he had cut away from the injured man's swollen ankle.

Lovett assigned three detectives—Bernard Adamson, Aquilla Allen, and Wallace Kirby—to hide in the trees near the Mudd home and keep watch on the chance that Booth might reappear. Lovett was convinced Booth was hiding somewhere in Zekiah Swamp and would soon return to Mudd's house seeking medical aid for his broken leg. The three men were left with instructions to shoot anyone who appeared. Outwardly, the War Department was saying Booth should be brought back alive, but historians are convinced Stanton secretly wanted him dead.

According to Balsiger and Sellier, around mid-morning on Easter Sunday, NDP detectives William Bernard and Ernest Dooley found David Herold sleeping along the side of the road leading to Hughesville, Maryland. Bernard recognized Herold as an accomplice of Booth's and immediately placed him under arrest. Herold was taken back to Washington for questioning.

When Lafayette Baker arrived in Washington in response to the official request, he was taken directly to the offices of the secretary of war. Here, he found a panicked Stanton begging for help and explaining that Booth had to be found and quickly. If allowed to escape, said Stanton, the actor could identify a number of highly placed people as plotters and traitors and many would be ruined. If Booth could be found before such a thing happened, however, everyone involved in the capture would receive hefty rewards.

Baker quickly organized a team of investigators. He informed his charges that Stanton had put up $200,000 in reward money to be split among the team should Booth be captured.

Baker ordered one group of troopers to Benedict's Landing to see what they could find out. He also sent three men to Port Tobacco to search for Booth. Baker also arranged for a boat, the *Jenny B*, to cruise up and down the Potomac River and intercept all suspicious craft. During this patrol, the officers encountered an old Negro who said he saw two men resembling Booth and Herold entering a small boat to cross the river. One of the men, he said, was lame.

Meanwhile, David Herold was delivered to NDP headquarters for questioning. While Herold was held in confinement, Baker, according to Balsiger and Sellier, was meeting with Luther Potter, Andrew Potter, and Whippet Nilgai, a well-known Indian tracker who had worked with the government on several occasions. Baker unrolled some maps and showed Nilgai a number of suspected routes Booth might have taken after crossing into Virginia. Baker explained that secret operatives had already infiltrated most of southern Maryland searching for clues to Booth's whereabouts.

Nilgai was to accompany NDP operatives Luther and Andrew Potter. Baker ordered the three men to find Booth before he was captured by civilian authorities, and he was to be taken dead or alive.

After the Potters and Nilgai departed, Colonel Everton J. Conger entered Baker's office with a rough sketch of a reward poster. The two men briefly discussed the pursuit efforts and the reward money. Baker confided in Conger that he wanted Booth dead. If the actor tells everything he knows to the wrong people, said Baker, a lot of high-placed officials were going to hang.

The conversation between Baker and Conger was interrupted by a soldier who entered the room and informed Baker that David Herold had been captured and was waiting outside.

Herold was brought into Baker's quarters and seated in a chair. Threatening the young man with hanging, Baker got Herold to admit he was involved in the kidnapping plans, but not with the assassination. When it became clear that Herold knew about Booth's planned escape route, Baker told him pointedly that if he led authorities to the assassin, his life would be spared. If he refused, he would be killed.

Herold, naturally, agreed to cooperate.

During the time Herold was in custody, authorities, acting on information they found in Booth's trunk, arrested Sam Arnold in Fort Monroe, Virginia. Under interrogation, Arnold implicated Michael O'Laughlin and Ned Spangler, both of whom were arrested shortly thereafter.

Around 10:30 P.M., Major H.W. Smith led several soldiers to the Surratt boardinghouse where they placed under arrest Mrs. Surratt, her daughter Anna, her cousin, and a young boarder named Honora Fitzpatrick.

The boardinghouse of Mary Surratt (Library of Congress photo)

As the women were taken into custody, a tall man, "built like a young ox," appeared at the front door. He was wearing mud-caked workman's clothes and was carrying a pickaxe. When asked his business by the officers, he glared at them and said had been hired by Mrs. Surratt to dig a trench. He was there, he claimed, to find out when he could begin work in the morning. When Mrs. Surratt was called on to identify the newcomer, she appeared alarmed, threw up her hands, and vehemently denied ever seeing him before and certainly did not hire him. The man was immediately relieved of his pickaxe and arrested. When asked his identity, he pulled out an Oath of Allegiance and handed it to the officers.

The name on the oath was Lewis Paine.

Paine was taken to General Augur's headquarters and interrogated but continued to maintain he was little more than a ditch-digger. William Bell, Seward's black servant, was brought in and, without hesitation, identified Paine as the man who assaulted the secretary of state. Paine was placed in double shackles and imprisoned aboard the navy monitor *Saugus* where his interrogation continued with Major Thomas Eckert. Later, when questioned by Lafayette Baker, Paine denied any knowledge at all of the attack on Seward. Furthermore, he denied any involvement with Booth's plan to kidnap or kill the president, vice president, and secretary of state. (See Appendix C, The Lewis Paine/Lewis Thornton Powell Controversy.)

According to Balsiger and Sellier, after Paine was led away, Baker summoned an NDP detective and ordered him to have a reward poster made up and distributed, a poster containing an image and description of Booth. The poster was to declare a $30,000 reward for the assassin. At the bottom of the poster, Baker continued, was to be a description of and reward for Lewis Paine. When the detective asked Baker why a reward was being offered for a man already in custody, Baker refused to respond.

Six of the eight conspirators (Arnold, O'Laughlin, Paine, Mary Surratt, and Spangler, and a man named Benjamin Ficklin) were now in custody on the *Saugus* and the *Monitor.* Herold was still in the custody of the NDP. It was determined a few days later that Ficklin had nothing to do with the plot, and he was released.

Only John Surratt and John Wilkes Booth remained at large.

Around noon on Monday, a contingent of soldiers led by Lt. Lovett and aided by ace tracker William Williams rode to Surrattsville and arrested John Lloyd. For two days, Lloyd was questioned while hanging by his thumbs from a tree. A notorious alcoholic, Lloyd was also denied liquor. Eventually, the tavern keeper talked, stating that he had turned over guns and liquor to the two men who had come to the tavern, men fitting the descriptions of Booth and Herold. Lloyd's information sent Lovett riding toward Bryantown.

In addition to being shackled and chained, each of the prisoners aboard the vessels had a canvas bag placed over their head, a bag that was securely tied around the neck. Small holes were cut into the sacks to facilitate breathing and eating. It is believed the prisoners were separated so they could not speak with one another.

Before being transferred from the ships to the Washington Penitentiary to await trial, the hoods, under orders from Stanton, were replaced with tight-fitting bags which, according to Roscoe, fit the heads of the prisoners like the gas masks used during World War II and the Korean War. The new hoods were eyeless and possessed only slits for the nose and mouth. The prisoners also had their ears stuffed with cotton. The intention of this new device was to keep each of them from seeing, hearing, or speaking. In addition, the prisoners were chained to seventy-five-pound balls.

The cruel and brutal methods of securing the prisoners shocked even the soldiers who were assigned to guard them. Prison surgeon Dr. George Loring Porter protested this method to Stanton, claiming the tight-fitting hoods would cause the prisoners to lose their minds or suffocate. Only Mary Surratt's hood was removed. Years later Samuel Arnold wrote that the headpieces were actually *tightened* on the rest of the prisoners.

During his incarceration, Lewis Paine confessed to attacking Secretary of State Seward. Many researchers believe he confessed so that he would be relieved of the torture of the hood, but it was for naught.

On Monday morning, 17 April, a very nervous David Herold led Andrew Potter, Luther Potter, Whippet Nilgai, and four other detectives into southern Maryland. The previous evening, Baker had coached the terrified young man to claim they were all friends of John Wilkes Booth and were trying to find him so they could help him escape.

The ruse was not particularly effective. The first time it was used, the man who was being questioned was so insulted and infuriated at the suggestion he might be hiding the assassin that he exploded in a rage and threatened the party with a rifle.

After riding away, Andrew Potter decided to try another approach. Potter knew that James William Boyd had been working undercover for the NDP and believed the secret operative could help them find Booth. Potter also knew that Boyd, after fleeing Washington, was hiding at the Maryland farm of Colonel Frank Beale. Boyd worked for a short time at the Beale farm as part of his recent undercover operations in the area. On arriving at the Beale residence, Potter found Boyd and explained their mission to him. Boyd, fearing even more involvement with the Federals, refused to help them. When Potter threatened to arrest Boyd for the murder of Watkins, the former Confederate officer finally relented and agreed to cooperate.

About an hour later, Boyd was tying his gear behind his saddle. After mounting up, he joined the Potter party as they rode away from the Beale farm.

About one mile away, Andrew Potter spotted a farmhouse some fifty yards off the main road. Boyd explained to Potter that the farmer living there was a Confederate sympathizer and might be worth questioning. While the detectives waited, Boyd and Herold rode up to the house. As they made their way slowly along the tree-lined lane, the two men engaged in conversation and discovered they were both Southern men and were being shamelessly used by the Yankees. Before much distance was covered, the two agreed to attempt an escape at the first possible opportunity.

Thirty minutes later, Boyd and Herold returned to the point in the road where the detectives waited, stating they had no luck at the farmhouse. The group turned down the road and headed for Port Tobacco.

In the pine thicket near the Cox farm, Booth continued nursing his wounded leg. From time to time, he wrote in his journal.

During one spate of writing, Booth rationalized his role in the assassination and blamed others for weakness. Painting himself as a hero, Booth wrote that the "...country owed all her troubles to [Lincoln], and God simply made me the instrument of His punishment."

Throughout Washington and parts of Maryland, wanted posters engineered by Lafayette Baker were being tacked up. Oddly, the description of Booth contained little substantive information, no mention of his moustache, and the entire description totaled only forty-two words:

> Height 5 feet 8 inches; weight 160 pounds; compact build; hair jet black, inclined to curl, medium length, parted behind; eyes black, and heavy dark eye-brows; wears a large seal ring on little finger; when talking inclines his head forward; looks down.

To this day no one can explain why, when more complete details of Booth's appearance were available, the circular provided information that was of little use and partly misleading. According to Booth's sister, Asia, the actor's eyes were hazel. Why the contrived description was placed on the poster remains a mystery even now.

By contrast, the description of Lewis Paine, who was already incarcerated at the time, was incredibly detailed and totaled 160 words.

Late Tuesday afternoon, the NDP detectives, Boyd, and Herold set up camp just off the road. Following a late dinner, they all wrapped up in their bedrolls and fell asleep near the campfire.

According to Balsiger and Sellier, Boyd awoke around 2:00 A.M. After looking around the camp and determining the detectives were sound asleep, he quietly awakened Herold and cautioned him to silence. Slipping noiselessly from the blankets, they managed to take one Spencer carbine and three pouches containing full magazines. Without disturbing anyone, they crept away into the darkness.

When the detectives awoke the next morning they discovered Boyd and Herold gone. Without pausing for breakfast, they mounted up and rode to the nearest headquarters to report the loss of the prisoners.

After sending a message to Washington alerting Baker to the escape, the detectives determined to continue on with their assignment. Luther and Andrew Potter followed the trail left by Boyd and Herold; the others rode to Bryantown to try to find Booth.

Within a short time, the Potters, along with ten other detectives, were assigned to the *Jenny B* as it patrolled the Potomac. At one point, the vessel was called in to the nearest port where a message from Baker was delivered to the operatives. The message stated that Booth was traveling with a male companion and that the two were likely hiding somewhere near the shore waiting to board a ship. The ship, however, could wait no longer and finally departed.

Andrew Potter decided both pairs of men—Booth and Henson as well as Boyd and Herold—had already crossed the Potomac River and were in Virginia. After studying maps, the Potter brothers decided that the only logical route Booth and his companion could take to cross the river would be from Chapel Point near Port Tobacco to Lower Cedar Point on the Virginia side, a distance of approximately ten miles. The Virginia site was between Mathias Point and the mouth of Machodac Creek four miles to the south.

Detectives Bernard and Dooley were provided with Spencer carbines, pistols, and plenty of ammunition and dropped off from the *Jenny B* at Mathias Point and told to patrol the roads. Andrew Potter and several other detectives were taken farther downstream to St. Mary's City where they leased riding mounts. From there, they undertook a concentrated search for the fugitives.

While all of these preparations were going on, the truth was that none of the men in question had yet crossed the Potomac. In fact, Boyd and Herold were hiding in the southern Maryland woods not far from the point were Booth and Henson had taken refuge near the Cox farm. Unknown to one another, each pair had decided to cross the river, go to Gambo Creek, and proceed on to Port Conway located on the bank of the Rappahannock River. From there, they would cross to Port Royal on the other side.

While Booth and Henson waited in the pine thicket, Thomas Jones continued to bring them food, liquor, and newspapers. During the evening of Tuesday, 18 April, Jones stopped at the Brawner Hotel in Port Tobacco for a drink. While there, he was approached by a federal officer who identified himself as Captain Williams. After asking Jones a few questions, Williams informed him that the government was offering a reward of $100,000 for information leading to the capture of John Wilkes Booth. Jones was tempted, but his loyalty to the South was unswerving.

When Jones left the hotel, he noted he was being followed. Everywhere he turned in Port Tobacco, he encountered detectives and cavalrymen, all searching and making inquiries. Jones' own house had been entered and searched. Fearing he was being observed, Jones did not take supplies to the pine thicket that night.

Meanwhile, Booth was growing more and more uncomfortable in his hiding place. The cold and dampness aggravated his wound, which was growing more painful by the hour. When Jones finally arrived the following day, Booth insisted he take him across the river, but Jones told the actor the river was being patrolled and all access points were closely watched.

On Thursday, 20 April, another reward poster was released, this one offering $50,000 for the "murderer" of the president. Booth's name was not mentioned, no picture of him appeared on the poster, and only a brief description of the actor was included, part of which mentioned that he wore a "heavy, black mustache." On the same poster were $25,000 rewards for John Surratt and David Herold. Herold was described as a chunky little man, very young, and wearing a thin mustache. Herold, in fact, had been in NDP custody since 16 April.

Yet another poster featured what were supposed to be photographs of Booth, Surratt, and Herold. The photograph of Herold, according to Roscoe in *The Lincoln Assassination*, was "a schoolboy portrait that bore little resemblance to the way he looked in 1865." The photo reportedly had been obtained from Herold's mother, who removed it from a family album. The image purportedly of Surratt was clearly a picture of someone else. It was later identified as his older brother, Isaac Surratt, who was at the time serving in the Confederate army in Texas.

Both Herold's and Surratt's names were misspelled.

A short time later, a revised wanted circular was produced under orders from Baker, presumably after the flaws were identified in the previous one. The revised poster was placed on file and only seen by the public after the trials of Atzerodt, Herold, Paine, and Mary Surratt. The revised poster contained a photograph of David Herold that was taken *after he was captured by the NDP on 16 April*. The new photograph of John Surratt was made well after 20 April 1865, the date indicated on the poster!

One week following the assassination, Thomas Jones was purchasing supplies at a store in Allen's Fresh, located some two-and-a-half miles east of his farm where Zekiah

Reward poster issued by Secretary of War Stanton six days after the assassination (Library of Congress photo)

Swamp ends and the Wicomico River begins. While he was selecting goods, a half-dozen or so cavalrymen rode into town, entered the store, bought drinks, and sat around a table conversing. A few moments later, a scout rode up, approached the soldiers, and told them he had just learned their quarry had been spotted in St. Mary's County, about twelve miles east of where they sat.

The troopers guzzled their drinks, mounted their horses, and rode toward St. Mary's County. Looking around, Jones determined there were no soldiers left in town. He decided it was time to get Booth and Henson across the river.

On Friday evening, it was dark when Jones entered the pine thicket and signaled the fugitives. When he was admitted, he informed Booth of what had transpired in Allen's

Fresh and told him the time to make a break for freedom was now, tonight.

Jones and Henson helped Booth onto Jones' horse, and together the three left the thicket. For two hours they traveled through the darkness, stopping once to eat. It had been cloudy and foggy the entire day, and as the night progressed, Jones later wrote, the "clouds seemed to grow denser and the dampness more intense." Finally, they arrived at Dent's Meadow near the Potomac River. Dent's Meadow was a rather secluded spot located behind Jones' farm and about one-and-a-half miles north of Pope's Creek. The meadow was, in fact, a narrow valley located between relatively high and thickly wooded cliffs. A stream flowed through the meadow, widening gradually as it neared the Potomac River. In some tall marsh grass near a grove of trees, Jones retrieved the twelve-foot long flat-bottomed boat hidden earlier by Henry Woodland. Jones pulled the boat to the shoreline.

Booth was helped into the stern by Jones, given an oar, and told to use it as a rudder. In the boat next to him were placed two seven-shot revolvers. In his belt, Booth carried the large knife. He still clung to his crutches. Henson was directed toward the bow where he seated himself and grabbed two oars. By candlelight and using a compass, Jones conferred a moment with Booth, directing him to a point far across the wide river. He cautioned Booth to stay with the compass direction and they would arrive at the mouth of Machodac Creek. Once there, they should be able to see a house nearby. Jones told Booth to introduce himself to the woman who lived there, a Mrs. Quesenberry, tell her he was sent by the farmer, and she would hide him.

Booth thanked Jones and handed him a wad of money. Jones took eighteen dollars—the cost of the boat—and handed the rest back to Booth.

A moment later, with Henson rowing, the boat disappeared into the inky blackness that descended on the Potomac River.

While Booth and Henson were attempting to cross the Potomac River in the darkness, Boyd and Herold were picking their way through woods and swamp in an attempt to reach a location on the Maryland side just west of Mathias Point, Virginia, where they had located a boat and intended to make a crossing.

For the first few minutes, Henson found the rowing relatively easy. After crossing about one-third of the river, however, the boat was pulled along by the extremely strong tide. Henson fought the current with all this strength, but about ninety minutes later, the two men landed back on the Maryland shore in Nanjemoy Cove.

Henson helped Booth out of the boat and then pulled the craft into a grove of trees. This done, they located a suitable site to camp for the night.

That damp evening, while huddled with Henson, Booth wrote in his journal:

> After being hunted like a dog through swamps, woods, and last night chased by gunboats till I was forced to return wet, cold and starving, with every man's hand against me, I am here in despair. And why? For doing what Brutus was honored for—what made Tell a hero . . . . I have only heard of what has been done (except what I did myself) and it fills me with horror. . . . To-night I will once more try the river with the intention to cross; though I have a greater desire and almost a mind to return to Washington, and in a measure clear my name, which I feel I can do. Tonight I try to escape these bloodhounds

> once more . . . . I have too great a soul to die like a criminal . . . . I do not wish to shed a drop of blood, but I must fight the course. 'Tis all that's left me.

This portion of the diary has long puzzled researchers. How did Booth believe it was possible he could clear his name? It is believed the only way he could have avoided the gallows was to implicate men in high office in the conspiracy to kidnap and kill the president. Several historians are convinced that Booth intended the passage as a hint, and that he intended to leave his diary where it might be found.

According to Balsiger and Sellier, Boyd and Herold successfully crossed the Potomac River on the evening of Thursday, 20 April, landing on the west side of Mathias Point. They moved quietly through the woods, passed Owen's Store before the detectives arrived, and made their way toward the farm of Dan Green. By this time, it is estimated that as many as 10,000 men—soldiers, naval brigades, and volunteers—were involved in the hunt for Lincoln's assassin.

About two hours later, the two men approached Green as he was cutting timber on the farm of William Spellman. The farmer immediately recognized Boyd, who was walking with the aid of a crutch. The two men, old friends, embraced one another.

Without bothering to introduce Herold, Boyd told Green his leg had been bothering him, causing him severe pain. Green led the newcomers to the shade of a nearby barn.

Boyd explained to Green that he wanted to get to Tennessee, and from there flee to Mexico. Until such time as they could arrange transportation, he asked if Green would hide them at his place. Boyd offered the farmer twenty dollars for his efforts. Green excused himself to tell Spellman he needed to go home. He returned to Boyd and Herold a few minutes later and led them to his house.

On the afternoon of 21 April, Lt. Lovett, accompanied by a squad of cavalry, returned to the home of Dr. Samuel Mudd and asked the physician to hand over the razor used by the visitor. Mudd did so and also informed Lovett of the boot he cut from the injured party.

Lovett examined the boot. It was from a left foot, and on the inside he found a portion of an inscription—"J. Wilkes____." The last name appeared to have been worn away.

Lovett showed Mudd a photograph and asked him if it was the man who visited his home. Mudd stated there was a "resemblance about the eyes and hair," but, he added, "it did not look much like the actor." It was, in fact, a photograph of Edwin Booth!

Lovett held up another photograph, this one of David Herold. The officer asked Mudd if it was the man who accompanied Booth. Mudd replied that it was not, that the photograph bore no resemblance to Booth's companion.

In response to another question, Mudd described the horse ridden by Booth. His description matched that of the bay mare Booth leased from the Washington livery stable.

Toward the end of the visit, Mudd stated he had grown convinced the injured man he treated in his home was, in fact, John Wilkes Booth. Lovett arrested Mudd and sent him under guard to the outpost at Bryantown. The boot with Booth's name inscribed in it was sent by courier to Washington where it was forwarded to the manufacturer in New York. The maker telegraphed the Washington operative that the boot had indeed been made for John Wilkes Booth.

During the afternoon of Friday, 21 April, Dan Green left Boyd and Herold at his home and returned to the Spellman farm to do some more work. When he returned Saturday evening, he found his wife visibly upset and complaining that the two strangers had been drinking and growing abusive. She pleaded with her husband to get them to leave.

When Green informed the two men that they were making his wife uncomfortable, Boyd begged his friend to be allowed to remain hidden on the premises for just one more night. Boyd offered Green an additional twenty dollars. Besides, claimed Boyd, his leg was paining him badly and he found it difficult to move.

Green took the money and agreed to let the two stay if they agreed not to upset his wife.

Late in the evening on Friday, 21 April, Booth and Henson made another attempt at crossing the Potomac River. The crossing was uneventful and they finally landed the boat on the east side of Mathias Point near the mouth of Machodoc Creek early Saturday morning. From there the two fugitives made their way a short distance inland and, about one hour later, arrived at the home of Mrs. Quesenberry. Here they were introduced to Thomas H. Harbin, Thomas Jones' brother-in-law, and Joseph Badden. Harbin had been one of the original members of the planter's group involved in a plot to kidnap the president.

While Booth and Henson were meeting with Harbin and Badden, Andrew Potter ordered the *Jenny B* pulled into shore at Mathias Point a short distance north of Gambo Creek. Here, Potter learned that some of his operatives were based at Owen's Store, apparently arriving shortly after Boyd and Herold passed it in the early morning.

Potter listened to rumors that the fugitives might be in the area. He determined that if Boyd and Herold made a successful crossing, then it was likely Booth and Henson did also. Potter selected four detectives, including William Bernard and Ernest Dooley, along with the scout Whippet Nilgai, to accompany him on a search toward the south. After acquiring necessary supplies and armament, the group set out toward Port Conway by way of Gambo Creek.

Harbin and Badden provided Booth and Henson with directions to the home of a Dr. Stewart, reportedly a man who might provide refuge and supplies. By sundown, the two fugitives reached Gambo Creek, a tributary to the Potomac, and located just north of Stewart's home. Needing to stop and rest, they hid in the dense woods alongside the creek. When finally ready to leave, the two men proceeded toward Dr. Stewart's home, leaving behind them in the campsite a number of articles, including Booth's diary.

Booth and Henson reached Stewart's house around 7:00 P.M. on 22 April and were disappointed to find the physician somewhat unsympathetic to their plight. Stewart was aware of the government's death sentence promised to any and all who harbored or aided the assassins. He provided the two men supper but refused to allow them to remain at his house. Instead, he directed them to the hut of Willie Lucas, a free black man, where they spent the night. During the evening, Booth, quite upset at the treatment, wrote a terse note to Stewart from loose pages apparently torn from his diary earlier:

> Dear Sir: Forgive me, but I have some little pride. I hate to blame you for your want of hospitality: you know your own affairs. I was sick and tired with a broken leg, in need of medical advice. I would not

> have turned a dog from my door in such a condition. However, you were kind enough to give me something to eat, for which I not only thank you, but on account of the reluctant manner in which it was bestowed, I feel bound to pay for it. It is not the substance, but the manner in which a kindness is extended, that makes one happy in the acceptance thereof. The sauce in meat is ceremony; meeting were bare without it. Be kind enough to accept the enclosed two dollars and a half (though hard to spare) for what we have received.
>
> Yours respectfully,
> Stranger.

On Saturday, 22 April, Andrew Potter and his party arrived at Port Conway. There had been no sign of either Booth and Henson or Boyd and Herold. Potter assigned Nilgai to scout the countryside to see if he could learn anything of the whereabouts of the fugitives.

About one hour after sunrise the following day, Nilgai returned to the temporary headquarters established by Potter. During his search, he found a place in the woods near Gambo Creek that had apparently served as a temporary campsite. At the camp, the scout found a number of articles including a pistol, a compass, two empty brandy bottles, a wallet, and a diary. Andrew Potter examined the diary for a moment and gasped in astonishment. It was Booth's!

Together, Andrew and another brother, James, also an NDP detective, read the entries. As they examined the book they were startled to read of Booth's meetings with influential politicians, businessmen, and military leaders including Jay and Henry Cooke, Thurlow Weed, John Conness, Everton Conger, and even Lafayette Baker! Tucked inside the diary, according to Potter's notes, were six photographs of women.

Andrew Potter, accompanied by detectives Bernard and Dooley, hurried back to the *Jenny B* where they encountered Luther Potter, and they showed him the diary. Luther informed Andrew that it had been learned Booth stopped at Dr. Mudd's house to have his broken leg treated and while there shaved off his mustache. He also told Andrew that Booth and another man fled into Zekiah Swamp. Luther said the man could *not* have been David Herold since he had been in custody at the time, escaping only Tuesday night with Boyd. Andrew deduced it was Ed Henson traveling with Booth.

Andrew and Luther discussed their findings. In the end, they decided not to return to Washington immediately, believing it was important to remain on the trail of Booth who they believed was heading south.

Andrew Potter entrusted Booth's diary to Bernard and Dooley and gave them instructions to deliver it personally to Lafayette Baker. They did so on the evening of Sunday, 22 April.

Long before daybreak, Sunday morning (23 April), Booth and Henson packed their few possessions and loaded them into Lucas' wagon. Lucas agreed to transport them through the woods toward Port Conway, about two hours away to the southwest, for ten dollars.

By now, the reward money for Booth, Surratt, and Herold totaled almost $300,000 and had lured a number of bounty hunters, who swarmed into the Maryland and Virginia area where the suspects were believed to be located.

General Ewing, Mudd's counsel, said: "The very frenzy of madness ruled the hour. Reason was swallowed up in patriotic passion, and a feverish and intense excitement prevailed. . . . "

Reports of Booth having been seen from as far away as Pennsylvania, Massachusetts, New York, and even Ohio, Illinois, Michigan, and Ontario, Canada, began to arrive at NDP headquarters.

Frank Boyle and William Watson, two civilians who bore a strong resemblance to Booth, were shot and killed. Boyle's body was taken to the Amory Square Hospital where an autopsy was conducted. Subsequently, it was buried in an unmarked grave at the Fort Lincoln cemetery. Watson's body was carried to St. Mary's City, placed aboard the *Jenny B*, and delivered to the Old Arsenal Penitentiary. Following an autopsy, the corpse was sewn into a canvas bag weighted with canon balls and dumped in the Anacostia River where it confluenced with the Potomac.

Sunday morning found Boyd and Herold aggravating Mrs. Green once again with their cursing and drinking. This time, she told them they would have to leave.

When Green arrived, Boyd asked him if he would take them to Port Royal on the Rappahannock River. Green said he was not able to leave, but a neighbor, a free slave named Willie Lucas, might be able to carry them to that riverbank town.

Following directions from Green, Boyd and Herold walked to Lucas' home, a rather squalid cabin in the woods. Lucas had some chores to do and was unable to drive the two men to Port Royal. Maybe in the morning, he offered. If not, he told them, his son Charlie could do it on the condition that Green accompany them. Boyd returned to the Green home and asked his friend to go along, offering him another twenty dollars. Green agreed, and Boyd and Herold walked back to the Lucas cabin where they spent the night in the nearby woods, one night after Booth and Henson stayed in the cabin.

About one hour before dawn, Willie Lucas drove the wagon into his yard, having just returned from delivering Booth and Henson to Port Conway. Since daylight was approaching, he decided to get busy on some chores. When it was light, Boyd and Herold approached Lucas and asked about transportation to Port Royal. Lucas told them he had work to do but his son Charlie would take them. A short time later Green arrived at the Lucas cabin, spotted Boyd and Herold already seated in the back of the wagon with Charlie Lucas at the reins, and climbed in behind them.

Young Charlie Lucas was confused. He could swear that the two men riding in the back of the wagon were the same ones his father carried to the river earlier that same morning.

Meanwhile, Major O'Bierne had picked up the trail of Booth and Henson after learning they had crossed the Potomac into Virginia. He immediately sent a wire to the War Department requesting additional forces to pursue the fugitive. Oddly, Lafayette Baker refused O'Bierne permission. Soon afterward, O'Bierne received strict orders to remain on the Maryland side of the shore. Some historians claim Baker neutralized O'Bierne so he wouldn't be able to share in the reward.

By 9:30 A.M., Monday, 24 April, Booth and Henson were searching for a way to cross the Rappahannock River near Port Conway. They walked along the north bank until they encountered the home of ferryman William Rollins. They told Rollins they needed to cross to Port Royal on the southern shore. Rollins explained the ferry was on the south side of the river waiting for the tide to come in so it could cross back. Booth explained they were in a hurry, but Rollins told them he had to go fishing.

About an hour later, Rollins returned from fishing and found Booth and Henson still hanging around the shore. He told the two men he would take them across, but at that moment they spotted the ferry on its way back and told Rollins they would take it.

Booth and Henson boarded the ferry shortly after it struck the north bank. Moments later, the craft, poled by Peyton Washington, was crossing back across the 300-yard wide Rappahannock River. After landing at Port Royal, Booth and Henson found a southwesterly leading road and took it.

About one mile from Port Royal, Booth and Henson met a black man leading two horses. Henry Johnson, one of Booth's accomplices, former valet, and sometime dresser during his performances, handed the reins of the two animals to the fugitives. Johnson's mother, called Aunt Sarah, worked for the Booth family for many years. Henry, likewise, had enjoyed a long employment with the Booth family.

Johnson and Henson helped Booth into the saddle. Johnson climbed up behind Henson and pointed the way to Fredericksburg, about twenty miles to the northwest. Booth and Henson turned the horses toward the city, riding a trail that paralleled the Rappahannock River.

On that same Monday morning, Andrew and Luther Potter, along with their contingent of detectives, breakfasted in Belle Plain on the Virginia shore, saddled fresh horses, and rode toward Fredericksburg. Luther was convinced that Booth had left his diary behind on purpose in

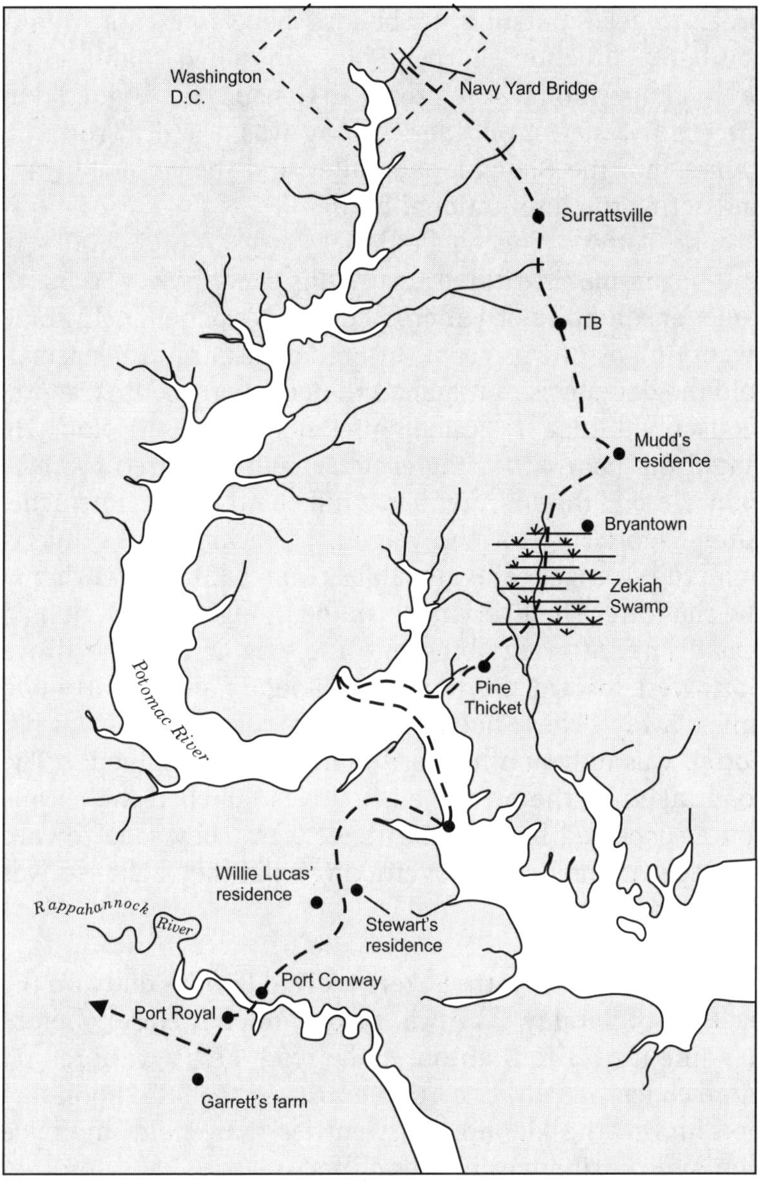

John Wilkes Booth's escape route.

order to lead pursuers to believe he was escaping in a southerly direction. Luther Potter reasoned that Booth's original intention was to escape to Canada. He decided that the road west from Fredericksburg was a logical route to depart into the Shenandoah Valley and thence northward and across the international border.

The Potters reached Fredericksburg around 9:00 A.M. and began making inquiries. By this time, however, Booth and Henson had not yet crossed the Rappahannock, some twenty miles downstream. In Fredericksburg, a liveryman told the detectives that he had rented a wagon late the previous night to a man matching Booth's description. He stated the man was using crutches and appeared to be in pain. He said the stranger had a full beard but no mustache. After negotiating for the wagon, according to the liveryman, the stranger called to a black man who was waiting in the shadows. The liveryman said he thought the black man was drunk. After climbing into the wagon, the pair drove northwest toward the town of Culpeper, about thirty-two miles away. The Shenandoah River, considered Luther Potter, was only another forty miles beyond Culpeper. The road taken by the presumed fugitives matched the escape route suspected by the NDP detectives. They rode toward Culpeper in the hope of overtaking what they believed was their quarry.

When Col. Lafayette Baker received Booth's diary on the evening of Sunday, 23 April, he examined it closely before handing it over to Stanton. As he read, he grew more and more concerned about certain entries in the little book that tied him to the kidnap plots, entries that could implicate him and possibly get him hung for treason. Baker did not trust Stanton to afford him any protection. Around dawn, Baker turned the diary over to Stanton.

The secretary of war, along with Rep. George Julian of Indiana, Major Eckert, Senator Zachariah Chandler, and Senator John Conness, gathered in Stanton's quarters reviewing Booth's diary. They were reeling at the implications of the information contained therein.

When all had examined the diary, Stanton placed it in an envelope and sealed it. He handed the envelope to Thomas Eckert and instructed him to place it in the safe and that it was not to be released to anyone under any circumstances without his, Stanton's, personal endorsement.

Rep. Julian remarked that it was one thing to hide the diary, but it was not likely they could silence Booth when he appeared in court. Stanton replied that Booth would never be tried in an open court.

While Stanton, Eckert, Conness, Julian, and Chandler were examining Booth's diary, Baker summoned his cousin, Lt. Luther B. Baker, Lt. Colonel Everton Conger, and Lt. Edward P. Doherty, and assigned them to tracking and capturing Booth. Baker was to lead the expedition, which included twenty-six mounted troops of the Sixteenth New York Cavalry.

Luther Baker and Conger were officers in Col. Baker's "Mounted Rangers," a battalion based in the nation's capital. Doherty was associated with the Sixteenth New York Cavalry.

Because Conger was the senior officer he would be the leader-of-record of the patrol, a courtesy command. Col. Baker, however, advised Doherty that he would actually be in charge of the pursuit and the acknowledged commander, but that his troops were also to be at the disposal of Lt. Baker. He instructed Doherty that he was to find Booth, capture him, and return him to Washington alive. Col. Baker showed the lieutenant a photograph of Booth and asked him if he recognized him. Doherty said he recognized the actor's image, but stated he had never actually seen him in person. Col. Baker handed the photograph to the lieutenant and told him to show it to his men so they would be familiar with their quarry.

Leading Doherty to a large map hanging on a nearby wall, Baker traced Booth's presumed escape route and stopped at Port Royal. Drawing a fifteen-mile-diameter circle around Port Royal, Baker told Doherty that Booth would likely be found somewhere within that area.

Doherty, Baker, and Conger, accompanied by the troopers, rode to the Sixth Street docks where they boarded the steamer *John S. Ide*. Around 4:00 P.M., the boat headed downriver for Belle Plain.

Tuesday, 25 April, O'Bierne received information that a crippled man hobbling along on a crutch and accompanied by a younger man had been spotted near the edge of a swamp two miles north of Bryantown! Accompanied by Captain Beckwith, O'Bierne raced to Bryantown, picked up the trail, but lost it in a dense pine thicket. The two men, according to witnesses, resembled Booth and Herold. It was subsequently determined this was a diversionary tactic to throw pursuers off the trail.

Shortly after noon, young Charlie Lucas pulled the wagon carrying Boyd, Herold, and Green up to the ferry at Port Conway. While Boyd struggled out of the wagon, Herold passed some money to Dan Green and the driver. As Lucas and Green pulled away, Herold walked up to the ferry operator, Rollins, and made arrangements to cross the river. Rollins helped Boyd into the boat, Herold followed, and the trip across the Rappahannock was made without incident.

On reaching the south bank, Rollins assisted Boyd out of the boat. As the crippled man and Herold made their way up the bank, they were met by three mounted men dressed in Confederate uniforms. They were A.B. Bainbridge, Mortimer B. Ruggles, and W.S. Jett. There is some confusion with regard to the actual military ranks of these three soldiers. At various times, ranks ranging from private to major have been designated. According to some documents, Jett, only eighteen years old, once served as a captain in the Confederate army, but gave it up when he joined Mosby's irregulars. Ruggles and Bainbridge appeared to be not much older than Jett. It is believed Ruggles, who joined the Confederate army at a very young age, rose to the rank of lieutenant but, like Jett, gave it up when he joined Mosby. War Department records indicate that Bainbridge and Ruggles were private soldiers at the time of the assassination. The department lists Bainbridge and Ruggles as having once served as privates. Some researchers claim there is no record that Jett ever served in the regular army.

Herold approached them and introduced himself as David E. Boyd. Pointing to his partner, he identified him as James W. Boyd, told them he was wounded in action at Petersburg, and asked the three soldiers if they could help get them through the lines and deep into the South.

Ruggles stated later that the crippled man was dressed in dark clothes and wore a black, soft hat. Bainbridge also subsequently wrote that the older man wore "a dark suit of clothes . . . strode about on a crutch, and had a long unkempt mustache." He also stated that the man had the initials "JWB" tattooed on his right hand.

Jett told Herold that the only place in the region where a Confederate soldier might hide would be at Garrett's farm, about three miles to the south. The three agreed to take them there. Ruggles climbed off his mount and helped the injured Boyd onto it. Ruggles then doubled with Bainbridge, and Herold climbed onto the back of Jett's horse. Together, they rode southward.

The five men arrived at the Garrett farm, some six miles from the river, around 4:00 P.M. and were met by farmer Richard Garrett.

Jett introduced his fellow soldiers and "John W. Boyd" to Garrett. He explained the crippled man had been wounded at Petersburg and asked if he could remain at the farm to recuperate while the soldiers rode south to Richmond on a scout.

Garrett, who was known to aid wounded and hungry travelers, told Boyd he was welcome. As the soldiers started to ride away, Herold showed them one of his boots with a sole nearly all the way off and asked if he could go along to purchase a new pair. The troopers said they would ride back this way on Wednesday, but Herold told Garrett he would try to return earlier.

Garrett introduced Boyd to his wife, his sons Jack, William, and Richard, his sister-in-law Lucinda Holloway, and his daughters Kate, Lilly, and Cora.

Following the introductions, Garrett encouraged Boyd to rest himself on a porch chair while he prepared something to drink for him.

In Culpeper, the Potters' search party discovered that a man resembling Booth had arrived by wagon earlier in the day, a wagon driven by a black man. The pair continued on toward Sperryville. The description matched the one they heard in Fredericksburg, so the NDP party took off in pursuit, finally catching up with their quarry on the road a few miles out of Sperryville. The suspects turned out to be complete strangers.

As the Potters were interrogating the two men in the wagon, Booth, Henson, and Henry Johnson were only just approaching Fredericksburg from the southeast.

Chapter X

The Killing at Garrett's Barn

Late Monday afternoon, 24 April, Captain James William Boyd relaxed on the front porch of the Garrett home. He was visiting with Garrett's daughters Cora and Lilly, likely the only pleasurable moments Boyd had experienced in weeks.

According to Balsiger and Sellier, Boyd showed the little girls his initials, "JWB," which were tattooed on his right hand. They were delighted when he pulled out his gold watch chain and showed them the gold ring that hung on it, telling them it was a gift from his wife but it was too small for his finger.

Boyd also showed the little girls his watch, explaining how it was wound and how the key was attached to the 18-karat cover. He said that when the hour struck, it was so hard that it vibrated the watch.

On Tuesday morning, Boyd's pain had lessened somewhat. He wound his watch and placed it in the pocket of his vest.

Around mid-morning, Jack Garrett returned from an errand with news of Lincoln's assassination and information about the rewards offered for John Wilkes Booth and David Herold.

During dinner that evening, Jack asked Boyd if he had ever seen Booth, and the officer stated that he once saw him in Richmond during the John Brown raid.

Around the time Boyd and Jack Garrett were discussing John Wilkes Booth, the contingent of twenty-six cavalrymen led by Conger, Baker, and Doherty were riding toward Port Conway from the north.

Among the riders was Sergeant Thomas P. Corbett, nicknamed "Boston," and soon destined to go down in history. Corbett was regarded as somewhat odd by his fellow soldiers, and they referred to him as the "Glory to God Man" because of his constant evangelizing. Corbett was regarded by most who knew him as being mentally unstable.

During the early afternoon, Luther Baker found William Rollins, the ferryman, and asked him if he had seen a man fitting Booth's description. Rollins admitted he had, that he had ferried him and another man across the river the previous day. When Baker showed Rollins a photograph of Booth, the ferryman stated it resembled a man he recently transported across the Rappahannock, but that his passenger had no mustache.

Rollins also told Baker that, after landing on the south side of the river, his passengers visited briefly with a Confederate soldier named Jett and then rode away. In response to more questioning, Rollins told Baker that Jett often went to Bowling Green to visit a lady he was courting.

Thomas P. "Boston" Corbett
(Library of Congress photo)

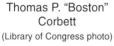

Baker asked Rollins to lead the troop to Bowling Green, but the ferryman refused, claiming that it would go poorly for him if it were known he was aiding the Union. Baker promptly placed Rollins under arrest and ordered him to serve as a guide. During the next hour and a half, the ferryman transported Baker, Conger, Doherty, and the entire cavalry contingent across the river. It took three trips.

Around three o'clock on the afternoon of Tuesday, 25 April, a pair of horsemen approached the Garrett farm from the southwest. As they neared the house, it became apparent that one of the mounts was carrying two riders. When the newcomers rode up to the house, David Herold slid off the rear of one of the mounts, thanked Bainbridge and

Ruggles, and joined Boyd on the front porch. The two Confederates proceeded up the road toward Port Royal.

Boyd introduced Herold to the Garretts as his cousin, David Boyd. After Herold showed Boyd the new shoes he purchased in Bowling Green, the two men began discussing plans for leaving the following morning and traveling to Mexico.

Approximately two hours later, Bainbridge and Ruggles were spotted riding at full gallop from the northeast. They pulled up in front of the house just as Garrett walked out onto the porch. The two men informed the farmer that a contingent of Yankees had landed at Port Royal and were heading in this direction. With that, the two soldiers rode away toward Bowling Green.

Boyd and Herold heard the warning. After the riders departed, they ran as fast as they could toward the woods behind the tobacco barn. Farmer Garrett was surprised at this reaction.

About one hour later, the troop of Union soldiers rode past the Garrett house on their way to Bowling Green. When the last of them had disappeared around a bend in the road, Boyd and Herold cautiously crept out of hiding and made their way back to the house. Concerned about their mysterious behavior, both the elder Garrett and son Jack approached the two and asked why they ran and hid when the soldiers approached.

Boyd tried to pass it off as a minor problem stemming from some difficulties he had with Union soldiers in Maryland. Both Garretts, however, were growing suspicious.

Later in the day, Jack Garrett was visiting a neighbor when he learned that the cavalrymen that rode past the house were hunting a crippled man accompanied by a young companion. He hurried home, rode directly up to Boyd and Herold, and told them they needed to leave before they caused problems for his father. Boyd asked Garrett if he could purchase a horse, but Jack refused.

Boyd agreed they should leave, but as it was now dark, he promised they would depart in the morning. Jack Garrett insisted the two men be gone at once, but he finally agreed to allow them to spend the night in the tobacco barn on the condition they depart at first light. Boyd handed Jack ten dollars for his help.

Jack Garrett led Boyd and Herold to the tobacco barn, pointed out a place they could sleep on the hay, and left them around nine o'clock. Once outside, Jack closed the barn door and locked it.

The barn was approximately sixty feet square and empty but for a few pieces of unused furniture and some loose hay stacked in one corner. The planks of the barn were of milled timber and nailed up such that four-inch wide cracks remained, the spaces allowing for the free passage of air to dry the tobacco when the structure was in use. In addition to the main door of the barn Jack had locked, there were, according to Provost Marshal James O'Bierne, at least two smaller ones that were fastened on the inside.

After locking the door to the barn, Jack Garrett walked into the house and handed the key to his aunt, Mrs. Holloway, explaining what he had done. Recalling the other doors, he told her that he feared the two men would try to leave the barn and steal some of the horses. He told her not to give the key to anyone but him. With that, Jack left the house, fetched his brother William, and together the two went to the corncrib where they spent the night standing guard over the barn and the corral.

Around midnight, Baker located Willie Jett at Bowling Green's Goldman Hotel. Baker, accompanied by Conger, told Jett they knew of his role in aiding "Booth" and demanded to know the whereabouts of the president's assassin and his companion. At first, Jett denied the charge, but Conger placed a revolver to his head as several cavalrymen filed into the hotel room. Visibly frightened and intimidated, Jett explained that he dropped the two men off at Garrett's farm.

Aware that they must have ridden right by the location, Conger ordered Jett to guide them back to the Garrett farm. Conger threatened to kill Jett if the information turned out to be false.

The cavalrymen, led by Baker, Conger, and Doherty and accompanied by Jett and Rollins, rode up to the Garrett farm around four o'clock, Wednesday morning, 26 April. After deploying the tired soldiers around the house, Baker stepped onto the porch and knocked loudly on the front door. Garrett leaned out an adjacent window to see what was going on, and Baker laid the end of his pistol barrel against the farmer's temple, commanding him to open the door immediately. Seconds later, Garrett pushed the front door open and, wearing only nightshirt and pants and holding a candle, stood facing the soldiers.

Conger stepped up to Garrett and inquired about the two men they knew to be on the premises. Garrett told Conger they left, that they ran away into the woods. Baker did not believe the farmer and had him led out into the yard. Garrett's hands were tied behind him and he was forced to stand on a chopping block placed near a tree. A rope was thrown across an overhanging limb and a noose looped around the farmer's neck.

Mrs. Holloway came out of the house and immediately took in the situation. When she spotted Jett she screamed at him for bringing the Union troops to the farm.

Baker, placing the point of his pistol into Garrett's throat, asked him once again to reveal the whereabouts of the two men. Garrett, now horribly frightened, stammered out a response that the Federal troops scared the men into the nearby woods when they passed the house the previous day.

At this point, Jack Garrett, having left his post in the corncrib and followed by his brother William, hurried onto the scene and shouted for Baker to wait. Pointing to the tobacco barn, Jack told him the men they wanted were inside.

Conger ordered several of the nearby troopers to seize the brothers, and while the elder Garrett was still standing on the block with the noose around his neck, they were pushed toward the tobacco barn.

Jack Garrett told Conger that the two men were locked inside the barn and that his aunt had the only key. A trooper was immediately sent to the house to retrieve it. Several soldiers were ordered to surround the barn and told that under no circumstances were they to shoot the suspects, that the fugitives were to be taken alive. When Conger received the key he handed it to Jack and ordered him to open the barn door.

Baker stepped up to the barn door with Jack and knocked on it with the end of his revolver. Receiving no answer, he told Jack to go into the barn, collect whatever guns were in there, and bring the two men out.

Garrett demurred, telling Baker that the strangers were armed. Baker shoved Jack roughly toward the door, and as he unlocked it, the NDP chief called out to the two men inside to hand their weapons over to the man coming in. Following that, he commanded they surrender and step outside.

All was silence outside the barn as young Garrett stepped into the dim interior. Seconds later, muffled conversation could be heard, then someone shouted, "Damn you! You've betrayed me! Get out of here or I'll shoot!" With that, Jack Garrett turned to leave, but Baker told him he couldn't come out until he secured all of the weapons. Garrett replied they wouldn't turn them over and, sounding anxious and frightened, asked to be let out. Finally, Baker opened the door and Garrett hurried out of the barn.

Baker called again to the men inside the barn to surrender, that they were surrounded by fifty soldiers and the structure would be set afire if they didn't come out.

From inside the barn, a voice called out, asking, "Who are you? What do you want? Who do you want?" Baker explained that he knew their identity, that he was placing them under arrest, and to throw down their weapons and come out.

The same voice called out again, asking who was out there and what did they want.

Conger stepped up and yelled that it didn't matter who they were. The voice inside said, "This is a hard case. It may be I am to be taken by my friends." After a few seconds of silence, the man in the barn said that if the soldiers would be led away, he would come out and fight the leaders one at a time. "Give me a chance for my life," he said.

Baker merely repeated his command to throw down weapons and surrender.

The voice responded, "Well then, my brave boys, prepare a stretcher for me."

Then more silence.

During the exchange between the officers and the man inside the barn, the cavalrymen had dismounted and led their horses away from the barn should it be set afire. The soldiers, exhausted from not having slept for at least two days and nights, dropped to the ground under the nearby trees for some rest. Conger prevailed upon six of the tired men to sit on some rails about thirty feet from the barn, rifles at the ready.

Conger then ordered Jack Garrett to pile some dry sticks against one wall of the barn, that they were going to set it on fire. Hesitantly, Jack carried an armload of kindling and stacked it against one wall. A minute later he returned to Conger and told him the man inside the barn threatened to shoot if any more sticks were set down.

Suddenly, the voice inside called out, "Captain, there is a man in here who wants very much to surrender." A few seconds later, Herold cried that he was coming out, that he was willing to cooperate. He said he was unarmed.

Baker told Herold to come ahead. The young man stepped toward the door and, according to Baker, said, "Let me out, quick. I do not know anything about this man." Cautiously, Herold extended his arms through the partially opened door. Baker quickly stepped forward, grabbed one of the exposed wrists, and jerked Herold out and onto the ground. The fugitive was immediately grabbed by Doherty and several troopers, and, as the youth begged for mercy, was led away.

From the moment he was seized and pulled from the barn, Herold maintained he was unacquainted with the man inside. Later, Doherty questioned Herold and said the youth insisted the man in the barn was named Boyd. When told it was Booth, Herold, according to Doherty, stated, "I did not know it; I did not know it was Booth."

Baker turned back toward the doorway and called to the man inside once again to surrender and come out. From within, the fugitive once again offered to fight, this time stating he would take on the entire cavalry troop.

Baker replied that such a proposal was out of the question and repeated his command for surrender. The voice asked for some time to consider the proposition, and Baker told him he would give him two minutes.

A few seconds later, the voice said, "Captain, I've had half a dozen chances to shoot you. I have a bead drawn on you now, but I don't wish to do it. Withdraw your men from the door and I'll come out. Give me a chance for my life, for I won't be taken alive."

Baker, maintaining his position, shouted, "Your time is up. We will wait no longer. We will fire the barn."

The voice responded, "Don't destroy the gentleman's property. He is entirely innocent. He doesn't know who I am."

As Baker spoke to the man in the barn, Conger instructed his charges not to approach the structure and reminded them that under no circumstances was anyone to fire a shot. Following this, Conger crept to the side of the barn where the kindling had been piled. After placing an armful of loose hay atop the sticks, he struck a match and started a blaze. The dry hay and wood caught instantly and began to spread to the dry barn timbers.

The dim light from the flames slightly illuminated the man inside. Conger saw him rise from a bed of straw and balance himself precariously with the aid of a crutch. With his right hand, the man raised a carbine and pointed it toward the growing fire. Anticipating that the fugitive might shoot, Conger immediately reached for his pistol, prepared to return fire if necessary.

The man in the barn took a step toward the fire, peering into the cracks of the siding as though attempting to catch sight of a target. He reached down, grabbed a small table, and appeared as if he intended to throw it at the blaze. After a moment he dropped the table, then his crutch, and moved the carbine from his right hand to his left. With the right hand, he drew a revolver from his belt and, noticing the main door of the barn was partially open, turned and began limping toward it.

Suddenly, a pistol shot was heard from the opposite side of the barn, and the man fell forward in a heap, rolling partly over. Reacting quickly, Baker, followed by Jack Garrett, jumped into the barn, twisted the revolver out of the man's right hand, and began dragging him outside. It was approximately 3:30 A.M.

According to Doherty, when he heard the shot, he pulled Herold over to where the wounded man lay just outside the barn, presumably to identify him. Herold reportedly asked Doherty who the man was. The lieutenant replied, "You know who it is." Herold stated that he did not, and was only aware that the man's name was Boyd.

As Jack Garrett was calling for help to put out the fire, Conger ran around to the front of the barn as the wounded man was pulled outside. Baker asked Conger why he had shot him. Looking down at the wounded man, Conger said it was Booth and that he must have committed suicide. Baker said no, that one of the soldiers must have shot him through a crack in the barn planking. Conger, however, continued to insist that he must have shot himself.

In subsequent testimony, Baker stated that he believed Conger fired the fatal shot, an action he considered odd since Conger himself gave orders that the suspects were not to be shot. Baker said, "If Conger shot Booth, it better not be known."

Baker and Conger, with the help of Jack Garrett, carried the body away from the growing heat of the blazing barn and laid it on the grass under some trees. As Baker examined the man, Conger and Doherty went among the troops trying to find out who fired the shot.

Eventually, Sergeant Boston Corbett stepped forward and claimed he had shot the man in the barn. Asked why he disobeyed orders, Corbett stated that God told him to do it. At this, Corbett's fellow cavalrymen began to laugh and deride. Not a single soul had witnessed the shot, yet none could believe that "Glory to God" Corbett, the former insane asylum inmate, could have done it. (See Appendix A, The Mystery of Boston Corbett.)

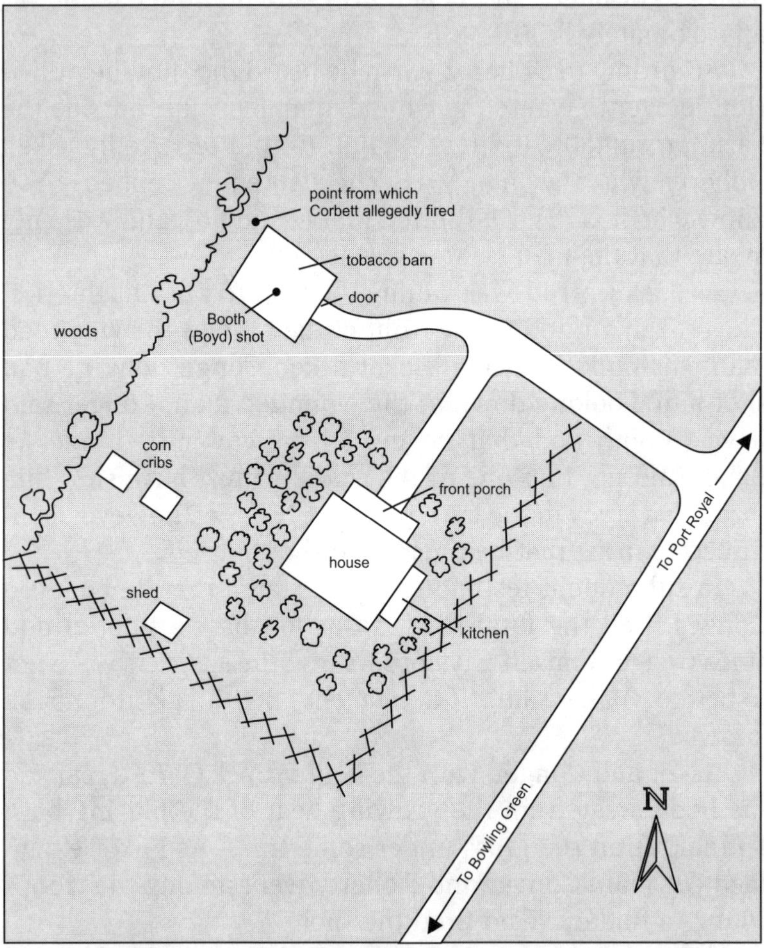

Map showing Richard Garrett's yard, farmhouse, and outbuildings.

Blood was streaming from the wounded man's neck. The bullet had entered the right side of the neck below the ear and followed an oblique downward course at an angle of about twenty degrees, penetrating three vertebrae and exiting on the left side leaving a noticeable hole. The ball had nearly severed the spinal column.

From where he still stood on the chopping block with the noose still around his neck, farmer Garrett looked down on the wounded man, who was wearing a Confederate uniform. Nervously, he asked Lt. Baker who it was, stating he thought he heard someone say it was John Wilkes Booth. Garrett told Baker the man gave his name as Boyd when he arrived the previous day.

On the grass, the wounded man was having trouble breathing and his body appeared to be completely paralyzed. In a halting, choking voice, he gasped out the words, "Tell mother... tell mother... I die for my country."

A mattress was dragged out of the house and onto Garrett's front porch. The wounded man was lifted from the ground and placed on it. A trooper was dispatched to Port Royal to find a physician and return with him.

As the man lay on the mattress, he caught sight of Jett. He turned slightly toward Conger and asked, "Did that man betray me?"

As he bled from the neck, the dying man's clouding eyes watched as Conger went through his coat pockets, removing a pocket knife, two pistols, an ammunition box, a compass, a handkerchief, a pipe, some tobacco, a bill of exchange drawn on a Montreal bank, a small amount of money, a file, and a leather-bound memorandum book.

The signet ring, always worn by John Wilkes Booth, was not found.

Clearly in pain, the wounded man muttered, "Kill me ... kill me." Baker looked at him and said, "No, Booth." In later testimony, Baker stated, "When I said 'Booth,' he seemed surprised, opened his eyes wide, and looked about."

The physician, Dr. Urquhart of Port Royal, arrived sometime later and after examining the wound in the neck told Baker that the ball had passed through the bones of the neck, "perforating both sides of the collar." He said the victim could not live another hour.

With that pronouncement, Conger scooped up some of the belongings of the wounded man, including the memo book, compass, and bill of exchange, and stated he was going to ride back to Washington and file a report with Lafayette Baker.

From the mattress, the wounded man was having difficulty breathing. He hissed, "Kill me! Kill me!"

Around 7:00 A.M., 27 April, the suspect died on the mattress where he lay. History has long recorded that it was John Wilkes Booth, but from the time he was dragged out of the burning barn, a great deal of confusion reigned and doubt was expressed regarding his actual identity.

Prevailing evidence suggests it was not John Wilkes Booth at all, but James William Boyd.

The events at the Garrett farm have been characterized by scholars as confusing and contradictory. Exhaustive research into the role of the government in the event reveals stunning evidence of secrecy, outright lying, conspiracy, and cover-up. Eisenschiml wrote, "Due to strange gaps and contradictory hedging in formal subsequent testimony, no senatorial inquest or ultimate historical inquiry could determine exactly what happened that night at the Garrett barn."

Perhaps not, but as more information becomes available, as the recorded events of the assassin's flight and ultimate death, as well as the subsequent events surrounding the body are examined in detail, it becomes shockingly apparent that John Wilkes Booth escaped and that James William Boyd was mistaken for the actor.

Chapter XI

The Body

Luther Baker was given charge of disposing of the body of the man killed at Garrett's farm. Still dressed in a Confederate uniform, the corpse was sewn securely into the horse blanket that covered him.

Baker needed a wagon to transport the body and asked Garrett if he had one. Garrett, who had been standing on the chopping block for over three hours, explained that he did not own a serviceable one. He told the lieutenant that a neighbor, a black man named Ned Freeman, had one. Baker sent two troopers to the Freeman cabin to secure the vehicle.

About one hour later, the wagon, an old army ambulance, was guided into the Garrett yard, driven by Freeman himself. The body was tied to a board and placed on the wagon bed. The saddle blanket was too short to cover the entire body, and the corpse's booted feet stuck out from one end.

Baker told Freeman the body was to be delivered to Belle Plain, about twenty miles northwest of Port Conway, where it would be loaded onto the awaiting steamer *John S.*

Ide. Lt. Baker, accompanied by one trooper, and the prisoner Willie Jett were to serve as an escort. The decision to have only a single trooper and Jett accompany the body to Belle Plain was curious, and one that has never been explained.

At approximately 8:30 A.M., the wagon and escort pulled out of the Garrett yard and proceeded toward the Rappahannock River crossing at Port Royal.

The remaining troopers, led by Doherty, followed several minutes behind Baker. David Herold was forced to run along beside a mounted trooper, a rope fastened tightly about his neck. Even as he struggled to keep up with the column, Herold continued to maintain his innocence, claiming he was only an accidental traveling companion to the dead man whom he continued to call Boyd. After traveling about three miles, Herold, after much complaining, was allowed to ride a horse that was procured for the purpose.

On reaching Port Royal, Baker, seemingly in a hurry, did not wait for Doherty's contingent to catch up. Instead, he had the wagon, the escort, and the prisoner loaded onto the ferry, and the Rappahannock River was crossed quickly and without incident.

About one mile out of Port Conway, the road forked. The right fork went directly to Mathias Point; the left fork wound across a seldom-traveled portion of King George County, eventually terminating at Belle Plain. Baker, Conger, Doherty, and the twenty-six troopers had ridden down the Belle Plain road on the way to Bowling Green the previous day, so the lieutenant was well aware that it was extremely muddy from recent spring rains and replete with deep ruts and potholes. Furthermore, the road snaked through a densely wooded wilderness, and there were no towns between the fork in the road and Belle Plain.

Baker was inclined to travel the better route to Mathias Point, but Freeman turned off the main road onto the narrower lane. When the lieutenant inquired, the former slave replied that he had taken this road to Belle Plain many times. Baker, anxious to let Lt. Doherty and the rest of the cavalry know of the route selected, sent the trooper back down the road to inform him.

Baker, Jett, and Freeman continued on.

Around early afternoon, the day grew warm and uncomfortable. The Belle Plain road was in bad repair and wound around and among steep hills. The wagon, already old and in poor repair, strained in the deep ruts and groaned on the inclines. According to historian Oldroyd, the wagon broke down around nine miles out of Belle Plain in a region known as Skinker's Neck, an isolated wooded spot adjacent to a pronounced meander of the Rappahannock River. A kingbolt broke and the front wheels slipped out from under the vehicle. The body in the back almost slid out.

Somehow, Baker found another wagon and, as Oldroyd wrote, "pressed it into service." According to subsequent reports and writings, the time that elapsed between the breakdown and the procurement of another wagon was three to four hours. During that time, the prisoner, Willie Jett, escaped.

Sometime in the late afternoon, Freeman steered the wagon toward an old steamer landing he knew of, and the party finally arrived at the shores of the Potomac River. Unfortunately, the landing had been abandoned for at least one year and was over half a mile downstream from the *Ide*.

Baker decided to ride upstream along the bank of the river to the steamer and get some help. Concerned that roving forces of hostile Confederates might still be in the area, he and Freemen hid the body in a nearby copse of willows. While Freeman waited with the body, Baker rode to the *Ide*, returning in two hours with two sailors. The body was loaded back onto the wagon and transported to the ship, finally arriving around six o'clock in the evening. The body was unloaded from the wagon, laid on the deck of the *John S. Ide*, and placed under guard.

About an hour later, the cavalry, led by Doherty and Conger, arrived and delivered Herold. He was immediately locked in irons, his head covered with a burlap sack, and placed in the hold of the ship.

Sometime during the following day, Herold made a statement to Judge Advocate General Holt and Special Judge Advocate John A. Bingham. The statement, strangely, was never released, and Herold was never allowed to be interviewed or even given a chance to speak in court. The conclusion arrived at by a number of researchers was that Herold possessed information the authorities did not want released. The educated speculation believes it had to do with the true identity of the man who was killed at the Garrett farm.

During subsequent questioning by Holt and Bingham, according to Eisenschiml's *In The Shadow of Lincoln's Death*, Herold maintained that he crossed the Navy Yard Bridge in the afternoon, not in the evening. Herold also insisted he was not with Booth when the assassin went to Dr. Mudd's house!

Later, say the interrogators, Herold admitted the man in the barn was Booth. Some are convinced this statement was either coerced or falsified. Eisenschiml contends that if Herold did indeed say the man shot dead in the barn was Booth, it was because he believed the real Booth had a better chance of escape. Eisenschiml also believed that for Herold to continue to insist that the man was Boyd would cause him to be ridiculed. Ultimately, according to Eisenschiml, Herold realized the authorities needed a dead Booth, so he gave them one.

Herold was isolated from the other prisoners and not permitted to talk to anyone. He was convinced that if he remained silent about the identity of the body, he would eventually be given his freedom. The naive young man trusted Baker and Stanton, not knowing they would never let him live.

As the *Ide*'s boilers were stoked for imminent departure, Andrew and Luther Potter arrived at the Belle Plain landing and came aboard. While searching for Booth near Fredericksburg, the two officers received word that the assassin had been shot at Garrett's farm. The report convinced them they had been following a false trail, so they packed up and returned to the *Ide*.

On boarding the vessel, the Potter's asked to see the body. Lt. Luther Baker led the brothers along the deck to where the corpse lay.

As two guards stood nearby, Baker pulled the blanket away from the corpse's face and the Potter brothers leaned over to stare. The two men looked down on a face that sported a long, shaggy, red mustache!

Straightening up, the brothers expressed shock and surprise and informed Baker that Booth's mustache was black and that he had shaved it off at Mudd's house only eleven days earlier.

According to Balsiger and Sellier, who quoted from Andrew Potter's personal papers, Baker was staggered by this news. He exclaimed, "My God! We got the wrong man!" The lieutenant then ran down the deck and off the boat, yelling for a fresh mount. He told the Potters he was going back to the Garrett farm, and the two detectives decided to ride along with him.

The three men arrived at Garrett's farm late in the evening and awoke the family by pounding once again on the door. When farmer Garrett answered, Baker told him they were looking for clues as to the identity of the man killed that morning. Garrett once again insisted that the man introduced himself as Captain J.W. Boyd of the Confederate army.

While Baker was interviewing Garrett, Luther Potter pulled his brother aside and told him that it was plain to see that the DNP had caught up with Boyd and Herold and mistook Boyd for Booth. Andrew Potter concurred.

Lt. Baker searched throughout the Garrett house but found nothing to help him with the identity of the dead man. He bade the Garretts goodnight and, with the Potter brothers, returned to Washington.

Meanwhile, Col. Lafayette Baker, in the company of Lt. Col. Conger, took a carriage to Stanton's residence. Baker was shown to the secretary's room, and when he entered he announced, "We have got Booth!"

Stanton, according to Baker in his book *History of the United States Secret Service*, placed his hands over his eyes and lay quietly for several seconds without saying a word. Then, he rose and very slowly pulled on his coat. Stanton, normally a man given to frenzy, explosive behavior, shouting, and even hysteria, one who was described as impetuous and would have been expected to respond excitedly, demonstrated an odd reaction to the information.

Stanton, in fact, reacted like a man who had just received some very bad news, appeared to be visibly troubled, and his eyes reflected fear and concern. Years later, Lafayette Baker wrote that Stanton "exhibited all the symptoms of a person who dreaded a deadly blow," and implied that he was concerned, perhaps afraid, that Booth had been taken alive! Stanton's apparent fear did not subside until Baker finally told him that Booth was dead.

The capital was rejoicing in the capture of Herold and the death of John Wilkes Booth. By the time they arrived, the Potter brothers decided they must inform Lafayette Baker of the true identity of the man killed at Garrett's barn.

Baker was stunned at the revelation, refusing at first to believe it. Luther Potter explained to Baker that Herold would be able to testify that the man who died at the farm was Boyd, not Booth. Baker, clearly worried, stated that Herold must never testify.

The Potters reminded Baker that Herold would surely be tried and that the information would come forth at that time. Baker repeated his promise that David Herold would never testify.

A number of researchers believe that up until the time David Herold was hanged on the gallows, the troubled young man was convinced the government had an agreement with him to let him go free if he kept quiet about the body that was being passed off as Booth's.

The ship bearing the corpse that was being identified as that of John Wilkes Booth sailed from Belle Plain to the Washington Navy Yard and anchored in the Anacostia River around midnight on the evening of 26 April. At 3:00 A.M., 27 April, according to Doherty, the body was transferred from the *John S. Ide* to the *Montauk*, also anchored in the Navy Yard. Herold, along with Jack and William Garrett, who had been arrested and charged with "harboring an assassin," was also placed aboard the *Montauk*. At the time Paine, Atzerodt, O'Laughlin, and Spangler were imprisoned on board the same vessel.

The blanket was removed from the body and the corpse was laid on the open deck, covered with a tarpaulin, and placed in the charge of a single guard.

Commandant J.B. Montgomery of the *Montauk* sent a telegram to Secretary of War Stanton informing him that the corpse was deteriorating rapidly and he requested instructions on what to do with it. There was no ice on the *Montauk* with which to preserve the body. Furthermore, it was clear to Montgomery the journey from Garrett's farm to the ship had been hard on the body. Stanton only replied that Montgomery was to allow no one on board the *Montauk* unless they possessed a joint pass issued by the secretary of war and the secretary of the navy.

Several historical references indicate Thomas Eckert, Stanton's aide, was appointed by the secretary of war to head an identification committee. Other sources say Surgeon General J.K. Barnes was in charge. The committee, which gathered around mid-morning of 27 April aboard the *Montauk*, consisted of Barnes, his assistant, Judge Advocate Joseph Holt, Special Judge Advocate John A. Bingham, Stanton's personal secretary William G. Moore, NDP Chief Lafayette Baker, Luther Baker, and Lt. Col. Everton Conger.

Alexander Gardner, noted Washington photographer, was called aboard to take photographs. A number of witnesses were produced, including: William W. Crowninshield, Charles Collins, Timothy H. O'Sullivan (Gardner's assistant); Charles Dawson, employed as a clerk at the National Hotel; Dr. John Franklin May, prominent Washington physician; a dentist named Dr. Merrill; and a lawyer named Seaton Munroe.

Curiously, extant lists of members of the identification committee and witnesses vary from researcher to researcher. The truth is, no one is exactly certain who participated, all of which adds to the growing evidence of confusion associated with the circumstances surrounding the body.

The charge given to the committee was to formally identify the body as that of Lincoln's assassin, John Wilkes Booth. Technically, it was an inquest. There was no autopsy performed.

The only thing the members of this committee had in common was that *none* of them had been personally acquainted with John Wilkes Booth. None of Booth's relatives were asked to participate in the identification and neither were any of his friends nor any of the kidnap and killing co-conspirators, many of whom were in custody aboard the *Saugus* and *Montauk*. "The corpse," wrote Roscoe, "bore little or no resemblance to the photographic portraits of John Wilkes Booth."

The first witness interviewed by the committee was William W. Crowningshield, a naval officer. During questioning, Crowningshield stated explicitly that he knew Booth to be five feet, nine and three-quarter inches tall. Booth was actually just under five feet eight inches. Crowningshield, however, expressed some confidence that the body that lay before him was that of Booth.

Another witness, Charles M. Collins, the signal officer of the *Montauk*, identified the corpse at 2:00 A.M. in the light of flickering torches. In spite of the dramatic changes that had taken place on the body and face, Collins, who did not know Booth, provided a positive identification in the dim light.

History does not record lawyer Seaton Munroe's qualifications for identifying Booth, and not a single researcher believes he had any. Munroe, however, stated that he was confident the body was that of the president's assassin. When Munroe was asked by Judge Advocate Holt if he recognized any special marks on the body, Munroe replied he recognized it "only from its general appearance." The fact is, the real Booth had several identifying marks, including a number of facial scars, scars on his arms and body, and the initials "JWB" tattooed on one of his hands.

According to one report, witness Dawson, questioned by Judge Advocate Holt, identified the body solely on the basis of the tattooed initials "JWB" on the "left wrist." Other official reports state Dawson identified the initials on the "right hand." Booth's initials, according to his sister Asia, were tattooed on the soft part of the hand between the thumb and forefinger. Thomas A. Jones wrote that he saw initials tattooed on Booth's right arm!

The tattooed initials should have proven to be an unmistakable mark of identification. Rather than settle the identity of the corpse once and for all, however, the various reported locations and descriptions of the tattooed initials merely added to the growing confusion. Earlier, Maryland provost marshal General J.L. McPhail, in a 26 April dispatch to Stanton, told the war secretary that Booth could be recognized by the initials tattooed on his "right arm" and a small cross on his "left hand between forefinger and thumb." Dr. G.L. Porter, an army surgeon who viewed the body, wrote that he saw the initials "JWB" tattooed on the right hand.

Booth biographer Francis Wilson wrote that the assassin possessed the "distinctive mark of identification . . . the initials JWB which were pricked in India ink on his right hand." Bainbridge, one of the soldiers who accompanied Boyd and Herold, stated some years later that he had noticed the initials "JWB" tattooed on Boyd's right hand.

John Wilkes Booth was right-handed. It seems logical that, using the hand he wrote with, he would have etched his initials on his left hand.

James William Boyd had the initials "JWB" tattooed on his right hand.

Dr. May was summoned to provide testimony. May was a distinguished Washington physician who, eighteen months earlier, removed a growth—a fibroid tumor—from the neck of a man he believed was John Wilkes Booth. May treated and stitched the resultant opening. Approximately one week following the surgery, the patient returned—the wound, he claimed, had been torn open during a play. May had to resew the wound and told the patient it would leave a scar.

May ignored several requests to appear and was finally escorted to the deck of the *Montauk* by Lafayette Baker, who asked the physician to identify the corpse. Within seconds after Surgeon General Barnes removed the covering from the face, May, looking down on the corpse, stated that the body bore no resemblance to Booth whatsoever, and he said he could not believe it was him.

Barnes asked May to describe the scar that was left on the back of Booth's neck. Without hesitation and without actually looking at the corpse's neck, May did so, and Barnes replied, "You have described the scar as well as if you were looking at it, and it looks as if you have described it, *much like the cicatrix of a burn than that made by a surgical instrument*" (author italics).

During his testimony at the conspiracy trial, Surgeon General Barnes stated that the body had a scar "upon the large muscle of the left side of the neck three inches below the ear," and again repeated that it "looked like the scar of a burn instead of an incision."

May later recalled that he eventually did examine the back of the neck and found the "mark," which he also stated resembled a burn. Interestingly, May makes no mention of the two obvious bullet wounds on the neck, which must have been very close to the "mark."

Subsequently, Dr. May provided a written statement relative to his examination of the body on the *Montauk*. In it, there is no mention that he examined the neck of the corpse at all. It must be pointed out here that the bullet that struck the neck of the deceased had torn it up significantly, causing many to believe a simple sutured wound may have been completely obscured or obliterated.

A few researchers suggest the "burn," as the mark was identified by Surgeon General Barnes, could have been a powder burn, resulting from a pistol being fired close to the neck. Such a burn would be consistent with suicide.

Though May and Barnes initially identified the location of the "burn" as being on the left side of the neck, Barnes stated during subsequent testimony that it was on the *right* side of the neck! Several other witnesses also mentioned the scar as being on the right side of the neck. According to witnesses, the man killed at Garrett's barn was struck on the right side of the neck.

May stated that the body possessed some of Booth's features but appeared to be "altered" and much older in appearance. (Boyd was 43, Booth 26.) The physician commented that he did not recall Booth's body being freckled as was that of the corpse. May also pointed out that the corpse had a mustache. Several days following his testimony, May wrote a letter to a friend stating that the mustache he observed on the corpse "was so long and untrimmed that the hairs curled into the nose."

In his statement, May observed that he had never seen a greater change in a human being than that between the healthy and vigorous Booth he knew and the "haggard corpse which was before me with its yellow and discolored skin, its unkempt and matted hair, and its facial expression, sunken and chapped by the exposure and starvation it had undergone." May also referred to the corpse's facial expression as looking haggard and "pinched with suffering."

These statements by May are puzzling. It is known that John Wilkes Booth was well fed by Thomas Jones while hiding out in the pine thicket. The man who was killed at the Garrett farm was provided meals for two days. Furthermore, it can safely be presumed that while a guest of the Garrett's and in the presence of ladies, he had ample opportunity for personal grooming. Yet, the corpse lying on the deck of the *Montauk* was "haggard," "unkempt," starved, and had a red mustache. This certainly could not have been the body of John Wilkes Booth, and some suggest it might not even have been the body of James Boyd.

Even more bizarre and in direct conflict with the physician's observations, Seaton Munroe was quoted as saying the corpse's "handsome countenance was unmarred by the agony of his lingering death." Munroe also noted that the corpse bore no mustache! Could May and Munroe have actually examined the same body?

Continuing with his report, May stated that the *right* leg of the corpse was "greatly contused and perfectly black from a fracture of one of the long bones of the leg." Booth had broken his *left* leg, specifically the tibia, about two inches above the ankle! Boyd's injury was to his right leg. Significantly, neither leg bore a splint such as Mudd provided for Booth.

In spite of the dramatic differences, May's testimony was concluded with the statement, "I have no doubt it is [Booth's] body." On close inspection, however, it is clear Dr. May's statement had been altered. In an apparent attempt at modifying the physician's testimony, several of his original words and sentences were crossed out and others inserted above! In addition, the word "scar" was substituted for the word "wound."

Following the identification of the body by the committee, Surgeon General Barnes removed the perforated section of the dead man's neck to keep as a memento.

The question of suicide was never addressed by the committee. Ultimately, the inquest amounted to little more than having as its objective the identification of the corpse as being John Wilkes Booth, regardless of the conflicting testimony.

Furthermore, not a single witness who had known Booth well and for a long time was ever called to identify the body.

Following the work of the identification committee, the body was photographed by Alexander Gardner, one of the members. Gardner conducted his work in the presence of War Department detective James A. Wardell. Gardner was allowed to take only one photograph and was quickly hastened to a darkroom to develop it. Wardell stood by his side the entire time, and when the picture was finished, Wardell took possession of it, along with the plate.

According to Wardell, the photograph resembled Booth "except the hair is longer... the mustache is shaggy [and there is] growth on the chin."

Moments later, Lafayette Baker took the photograph and the photographic plate from Wardell. In response to subsequent inquiries, the government denied that any photographs were ever taken of the body. Sometime later, according to Balsiger and Sellier, the picture became the personal possession of Secretary of War Stanton. To this day, no one knows what became of either the picture or the plate.

On the afternoon of 27 April, Clarence F. Cobb, a former schoolmate of John Wilkes Booth who had remained a friend for years, was asked by General B.W. Brice to go to the *Montauk* and identify the corpse there. On his way to the monitor, Cobb was stopped by Surgeon General Barnes, who told him his identification was unnecessary, that the body had already been identified. Barnes also told Cobb that Dr. William Merrill, a dentist, filled two teeth for Booth during the first week of April and that the committee noticed the new fillings in the corpse's mouth. The truth is, Booth was not in Washington the first week of April; he was out of the city from 1 April until 8 April. Furthermore, no testimony from Dr. Merrill has ever been found among the records.

During the identification process, a number of people were shown what was purportedly a photograph of John Wilkes Booth. They included bridge guard Silas Cobb, ferryman William Rollins, and several soldiers who were present at the Garrett barn. In each case, they identified the photograph as John Wilkes Booth. The photograph was eventually placed in an envelope marked with the name of U.S. District Attorney Dawson and included in the archives of the judge advocate general. Years later when someone examined the photograph, it turned out to be one of Edwin Booth!

While the corpse was on the *Montauk*, a lock of hair was cut from the head by one Dr. J.M. Peddicord. These same hairs were analyzed years later by a Dr. Muehlberger who declared they were "entirely unlike Booth's hair."

One can only ponder the significance of all the secrecy and deception. The inquest was clearly a mock affair, obviously biased, ineptly conducted, and lacked necessary thoroughness.

Stanton gave the responsibility of disposing of the body to Lafayette Baker, telling him to hide it where it would never be found. Enlisting the help of his cousin Luther, Baker and an enlisted naval man named Edwin H. Sampson (some sources say Stebbins) ordered the body removed from the *Montauk* late in the evening and placed in a rowboat. A moment later, according to many witnesses who observed from the shore, a heavy ball and chain were also lowered into the boat.

The body was removed without the knowledge of Commander Montgomery, a highly irregular procedure. Montgomery learned the body had been "suddenly and unexpectedly taken from the ship" from one of his officers.

Somehow, the news of the removal of the body spread throughout Washington, and a large crowd gathered along the shore. As hundreds of spectators watched, the sailor rowed the boat downstream and away from the *Montauk* past Buzzard Point and Greenleaf Point and into the Potomac River. Observers watched the progress of the craft until it disappeared a few hundred yards away into the gathering darkness of the evening.

Night fell as the boat neared Giesboro Point on the Maryland shore. Here, the boat was steered close to the bank among the rushes and reeds, a location where aged and sick military horses were brought to be killed, their carcasses dumped into the river. The air hovering above this site was putrid, stinking, and rank.

The boat moved along the river toward the location of the Arsenal Penitentiary, eventually reaching the walls of the structure, which rose from the water's edge.

According to George S. Bryan in *The Great American Myth*, an earthwork was constructed at this location during the late 1700s. In 1803 a small military post was established, and by 1817 it had become the Washington Arsenal. Eventually, a federal penitentiary consisting of some 160 cells was located here, the prison operating side-by-side with the manufacture and storage of arms and ammunition.

It was at this former penitentiary that the boat carrying the corpse arrived. Here, a wide door opened and Lafayette Baker tossed the stern rope to a man who appeared in the opening holding a lantern. As the boat was pulled close to the door, Baker told the man to help him lift the body out. The corpse was removed from the boat and placed just inside the open doorway. Baker and the sailor then climbed out of the craft and entered the building through the same opening.

According to Col. Baker, the three men lifted the corpse and, following the man with the lantern, carried it down a concrete hallway to a cell, purportedly a vault where ammunition was once stored. Major Eckert, who was present in the building at the time but not at the actual interment, testified before a House Judiciary Committee hearing on 30 May 1867 that the burial occurred in a "large room in the arsenal building . . . the largest room in the building . . . perhaps thirty feet square . . . possibly more."

In the middle of the room (some writers say corner), a concrete slab had been removed and a shallow grave excavated. The body, enclosed in canvas, was dropped in. Some claim the body was laid in a musket case and the name BOOTH printed on the underside of the lid. Dirt was shoveled and scraped in and the concrete slab replaced.

Assistant Surgeon General Dr. G.L. Porter was present at the burial and later wrote that two men "picked up the body . . . still in its wrapping of gunny sacking, and enshrouded in an army blanket, and deposited it in the shallow hole."

No one present actually saw the body.

Moments later, Lafayette and Luther Baker and the sailor left the penitentiary the way they came in and climbed into the boat. As the massive door closed behind them, the sailor rowed away.

Again, the secrecy surrounding the disposal of the body remains curious. Did someone fear the corpse would be disinterred and recognized as belonging to someone other than Booth? Stanton claimed the secret burial was undertaken "simply and solely for the purpose of preventing him from being made the subject of Rebel rejoicing."

A common practice during this time was to publicly display the bodies of slain leaders and notorious criminals. The disposal of the body the government claimed was Booth represented a noted departure from that practice.

Shouts and accusations of a hoax quickly reverberated across Washington and the rest of the country. Heady rumors abounded that the man taken from Garrett's burning barn was not John Wilkes Booth. The *Constitutional Union* printed that the so-called capture, death, and burial of Booth was a "fraud" and maintained that the assassin had actually escaped. The Richmond *Examiner* wrote, "We Know Booth Escaped."

Several days later, Lafayette Baker formally closed the case on John Wilkes Booth. Following that, he called for a meeting with the twenty-six detectives who had worked on the case. Each of the detectives was given a $5,000 bonus for their contribution, but only if they signed a form stating they had "no further interest in the Booth case."

Each man signed.

During the month of September 1867, according to Bryan, the War Department decided to tear down a portion of the Old Arsenal Penitentiary building and improve the grounds. These plans made necessary the removal of the body presumed to be Booth's, as well as those of Atzerodt, Herold, Paine, and Mary Surratt. The latter four were buried in the yard following their executions on the gallows for their participation in the plot to assassinate President Lincoln.

On 1 October all five bodies were disinterred and carried to an arsenal warehouse, a little-used building with thick walls, stone floor, and a heavy iron door. The warehouse was located on the eastern side of the parade ground, and inside the five bodies were reburied in a trench eight feet wide and six feet deep. According to documents, the body identified as John Wilkes Booth was placed at the extreme right.

On 15 February 1869 President Andrew Johnson signed an order to have Booth's body dug up and delivered to John Weaver, the sexton of Baltimore's Christ Church. The executive order came in response to a request submitted five days earlier by Edwin Booth.

On the afternoon of 15 February, men of the Ordnance Corps dug up the body, now in a pine musket box. The bodies of Mary Surratt and David Herold had been removed weeks earlier and handed over to claimants. The name John Wilkes Booth, printed in capital letters, was barely legible on the top of the slightly decayed box. (Some documents state the lettering was on the underside of the lid.)

Four troopers carried the box to an awaiting wagon provided by the War Department. Around 6:00 o'clock that evening, the wagon pulled up to the back door of the undertaking firm of Harvey and Marr, 335 F Street. Ironically, the alley in which the wagon halted was the very same one from which Booth fled on the night of 14 April 1865.

The old ammunition box in which the body had been placed was badly decayed as was the body within. The skin was dark brown and shriveled and the skull was detached from the neck. The undertaker's son noticed at the time only one shoe accompanied the body. According to historian Oldroyd, the body was formally identified by a dentist who claimed to have filled Booth's teeth.

As the body lay in the Harvey and Marr Funeral home, a number of people came into the funeral home and "positively" identified what they stated was a remarkably well preserved corpse as that of John Wilkes Booth, even though the body had never been adequately prepared for burial and was little more than a skeleton at the time.

A Miss Blanche Chapman viewed the body and described it as a skeleton with "little of the remains left, the flesh having all disappeared." She also noted there was now, associated with the body, "an old army shoe and boot cut open at the top." Strangely, additional footwear had appeared with the body between the time it arrived and when Chapman observed it.

The body was then placed in a plain coffin, carried to the train station, and delivered to Baltimore, arriving at 9:00 P.M. From the station, it was delivered to Sexton Weaver's quarters on Fayette Street. It arrived wrapped in two army blankets on 15 February.

News of the removal and delivery of Booth's body circulated throughout the area. On the afternoon of the 16th, a large crowd of people gathered outside Weaver's. Hundreds were allowed to view the body, which now reposed in a mahogany casket covered with a hinged glass plate in a back room of Weaver's. An article in the 16 February 1869 edition of the *Baltimore American* stated a "skeleton" with the "flesh all disappeared" was transferred from the box to a metal coffin. On one foot, continued the article, was an old army shoe, on the other was a boot cut open at the top.

During the days of 16 and 17 February, dozens of people came by to gaze at the body. In spite of the fact that only a skeleton lay in the coffin, many offered "verification" that it was, indeed, that of John Wilkes Booth.

One of those who viewed the body was Basil Moxley, a longtime doorkeeper of Ford's Theater and a man who knew Booth well. Years later, Moxley stated the corpse he viewed at Sexton Weaver's had *red hair* and was not that of Booth, but that of another man "forwarded to Baltimore by the government."

Moxley also claimed he had once been present during a meeting between Edwin Booth and a private detective wherein they discussed the subject that the corpse was not that of John Wilkes Booth, and that the president's assassin was, in fact, still alive! During the early 1900s, Moxley maintained that the burial of this corpse, whoever it had been in life, was arranged to pacify Booth's mother, and that the entire family as well as a number of friends were aware of the innocent deception. Moxley was adamant that the body delivered to Sexton Weaver by the government was not that of Booth. Moxley also declared that Sexton Weaver was involved in the deception and was quite aware that the body was not Booth's.

While the body was at Weaver's, it was also viewed by Colonel William M. Pegram, a childhood friend of Booth. In a written statement, Pegram related that the body was clothed in a dark suit and a long cavalry boot was still on the right leg and on the left was the other boot that had been cut to make a kind of shoe. At the time, Booth's left boot, which had been left at Dr. Mudd's house, was in the possession of the U.S. government.

Joseph Booth stated that if the body was indeed that of his brother John, it should have only one filled tooth in the head. A dentist was not present, but Sexton Weaver produced a dental chart. Charles Bishop, an actor who requested permission to view the body, reached into the mouth of the corpse and brought out a filled tooth and showed it around to all in attendance. This differs markedly from the report of the dentist named Merrill who allegedly examined Booth's teeth during the inquest four years earlier and found *two* fillings! Colonel Pegram also stated he saw only a single filling. A third examiner, one Henry C. Wagner, found only one filling in the teeth.

Rumors surfaced again that the body laid out on display at Weaver's was a substitute for Booth's. Several former Confederate officers came forward and, after examining the corpse, stated the body was not that of the assassin.

The body that lay in repose at Sexton Weaver's was eventually buried in Baltimore's Green Mount Cemetery. From all descriptions and available evidence, it was likely not the body of John Wilkes Booth and may not have even been the same body that was examined on the *Montauk*!

To confuse matters even more, according to the Greenmount Cemetery records there appears to have been two burials of the body. One occurred around midnight following the arrival of the body at Baltimore in February 1869. The second took place on 26 June of the same year. Those present during the February interment stated there were no services. For the June burial, services were held in the Episcopal church.

The controversy over the body has never been resolved. Washington officials, including Stanton and Baker, remained steadfast in their position that the body was, indeed, that of John Wilkes Booth. Given the circumstances relative to their involvement in the conspiracy, they could hardly have stated otherwise.

During the years that have passed since the event at Garrett's barn, however, a growing number of researchers maintain quite the opposite—that the evidence for the body being that of Booth is weak, contradictory, and lacks substance.

Many government files regarding the pursuit and capture of John Wilkes Booth, as well as information regarding the inquest, were hidden away and labeled Top Secret during the days following the inquest. Years later after the authorities were forced to open the secret files, many key documents were missing.

On 9 June 1893, as funeral services for Edwin Booth were ending in New York City, most of the interior of Ford's Theater collapsed into a pile of rubble. It has since been explained that the tons of filing cabinets and boxes provided too much of a strain on the floors. Destroyed in the collapse were records of the Army Medical Corps, including the surgeon general's reports of the inquest on the body the government maintained was John Wilkes Booth.

Chapter XII

Tracking John Wilkes Booth

While James William Boyd was dying on the front porch of the Garrett house, John Wilkes Booth, accompanied by Ed Henson and Henry Johnson, was escaping westward across the state of Virginia.

Following the farcical inquest aboard the *Montauk*, Lafayette Baker was growing concerned over the numerous reports filtering in that Booth was still alive. If true, thought Baker, the damage the actor could do to highly placed government officials was inestimable.

In order to pursue the leads relative to Booth, Baker called in Luther, Andrew, and Earl Potter and ordered them to follow up on reports that a man answering to Booth's description, accompanied by a white man and a black man, was seen passing through the settlement of Orange Court House by way of Fredericksburg.

Desperate for some concrete information about Booth, Provost Marshal O'Bierne was also sent to Fredericksburg on a tip that the assassin and two companions were seen in the area. When he arrived, however, O'Bierne found no real evidence that the men had passed that way.

After arriving at Orange Court House, approximately forty miles west of Fredericksburg, the Potter brothers interviewed a black man who, on being shown a photograph of Booth, said it was the same man who spent the night at his cabin. The stranger paid him five dollars, he said. Acting on leads, the Potters continued westward toward Stanardsville, about twenty miles away.

At Stanardsville, a merchant told the Potters that three men similar to the ones described by the detectives passed through town on Friday, 28 April. The merchant showed the detectives a barn in which the three men slept. Before leaving, he said, the three strangers purchased some food from his store, including a ham, some canned goods, and some oats.

The Potters traveled from Stanardsville a few miles down the road to Lydia where they encountered a widow who told them that the same men spent the night in her house on Saturday, 29 April. They paid for their room with the ham purchased in Stanardsville.

By this time, the Potters were convinced that their quarry was indeed, John Wilkes Booth, and that he was riding with Ed Henson and Booth's longtime valet, Henry Johnson.

To their dismay, the Potter's lost the trail at Lydia. In spite of riding several miles out from the town in different directions, they found no evidence of their passing.

On 2 May, as they passed through Lydia on their way back to Washington, the detectives were approached by a black youth about eight years of age. The lad asked them if they were still looking for the three men they inquired about during their earlier visit. When they admitted they were, the boy told the detectives he knew where the men had been hiding, and that his father brought them food and coffee. He would take them to the place, he said, for twenty dollars. The detectives paid the boy who immediately led them out of town.

The Potters followed the youth along a trail that wound back and forth across the bottom of a dry gully. Near the head of the gully, the boy pointed to a small cave approximately one-quarter mile away and said that was where the men spent several nights.

Luther and Andrew Potter went to the cave and found enough evidence to convince them that their quarry had, indeed, lain up here for several days. After questioning the young boy further, they learned the three men had spent approximately one week in the cave.

Back in the town of Lydia, the brothers paused to examine a map. Beginning at Stanardsville, they drew a nearly straight line that ran through Lydia, Elton, across the Shenandoah River, and to Harrisonburg, all locations they had already investigated. Looking closely at the map near Harrisonburg, Andrew Potter offered the notion that they didn't go far enough in their search. After studying the map, he suggested they travel on to the small community of Linville.

Once in Linville, they located a man named Louis Pence, a farmer who neighbors said rode a horse that was given to him by one of three strangers who had come to town a few days earlier.

During interrogation, Pence acknowledged he accepted the horse, along with some money, from a man who asked to spend the night at his farm. The stranger was accompanied by two other men—one white and one black.

When shown a photograph of Booth, Pence tapped it and said it was the likeness of the man who paid him the horse, except the man had no moustache.

After assuring the concerned Pence that he was not in any kind of trouble, Andrew Potter asked him what became of the three men. Pence told them he took them to meet friends near Harpers Ferry.

If Pence was correct, then Booth was circling back toward the east. Then it suddenly occurred to the detectives: Booth owned a farm which was located near Harpers Ferry on the Potomac River where Maryland, Virginia, and West Virginia come together. They made haste to that location. On arriving, they found no sign of Booth or anyone else, nor did they find any indication anyone had been there recently.

During the time the Potters were searching Booth's farm, the assassin may have actually returned to Washington. According to Eisenschiml, a man named Hill, a printer and friend of Booth, was walking down the capital's E Street when he spotted what appeared to be a woman hobbling on a crutch a short distance ahead of him. Hill believed the person was Kate Robinson, and he strode toward her to inquire about her injury. When she turned to face Hill on his arrival, the printer was startled to find himself looking square into the face of John Wilkes Booth! Booth subsequently fled.

Dressing as a woman was not foreign to Booth. His sister Asia once recalled that as a young man, John "dressed himself in a petticoat and draped a shawl around [himself] . . . . He put on my long trained dress and walked before the long glass, declaring that he would succeed as Lady Macbeth . . . ."

On another occasion, wrote Asia, her brother ". . . dressed in my skirts [and] . . . put on a tiny bonnet then in fashion and went out across the fields. The men took off their hats as they passed in their work . . . ."

Clearly, John Wilkes Booth demonstrated an early tendency toward adopting female dress.

The trial of those deemed as conspirators in the assassination of President Abraham Lincoln—George Atzerodt, David Herold, Lewis Paine, and Mary Surratt—proceeded swiftly. They were sentenced to die by hanging on 9 May.

Convicted as accessories to the assassination, Sam Arnold, Dr. Samuel Mudd, Michael O'Laughlin, and Ned Spangler were sentenced to the prison on Dry Tortugas, a remote island several miles west of the Florida Keys.

The selection of this location has long confused historians. Normally, prisoners such as these would have been confined in one of the federal prisons in Washington or New York. It has been suggested that Stanton wanted these four isolated from potential interrogators and secretly hoped they would die of fever. Michael O'Laughlin did, in fact, perish from yellow fever while incarcerated at Dry Tortugas.

As the weeks passed, the public reaction to the assassination, the trial, and the executions died down somewhat, but Lafayette Baker, along with Luther and Andrew Potter, remained concerned that the assassin was still alive and dangerous to those involved in the plot to remove the president.

On 23 September, Andrew Potter, along with NDP detective William Bernard, arrived by train at Harrisburg, Pennsylvania, for a hunting vacation. As the two men stepped off the train, the Harrisburg constable approached them and stated he had news that might interest them.

Pulling the detectives aside and speaking in a low voice, the constable told them that three men had been in town for several days and had left two days earlier. He told Potter and Bernard that he recognized one of the men, a Negro, as Henry Johnson, Booth's valet. The other two men, he said, had full beards.

The constable told Potter and Bernard that on the morning of 21 September, the three men boarded a train for New York City.

Realizing he was once again on the trail of Booth, Andrew Potter sought and found the train conductor who verified the constable's assessment. As it turned out, the conductor had known Henry Johnson for years. One of the other men, he said, walked with a bad limp and used a cane. When the conductor described the third man, Potter recognized him immediately as Ed Henson.

The conductor told Potter the three men got off the train at Philadelphia, so the two detectives immediately headed for that city. On arriving, they questioned the crew of the train and learned that the three men left that same afternoon, continuing on to New York City. There, however, the trail grew cold once again.

According to his papers, Andrew Potter accumulated enough information to suggest that Booth, Henson, and Johnson, along with Booth's wife Izola, lived off and on at the actor's Harpers Ferry farm from October through part of November 1865.

In November the three men, all wearing disguises, departed for Pennsylvania where Booth allegedly met with Kate Scott, a former lover. Scott, according to an affidavit she signed, stated Booth was indeed alive months after the killing at Garrett's barn and that he visited her in Pennsylvania. She also claimed she was pregnant with Booth's child. After leaving Scott's home, Booth, Henson, and Johnson traveled to New York City.

Nothing more was heard of the three escapees until the third week of December 1865. A few days before Christmas, Henry Johnson, carrying three valises, was spotted by a detective in the New York City train station. When he noticed the detective approaching him, Johnson ran and quickly disappeared into the crowd.

The same afternoon Johnson was spotted in New York, Booth's wife Izola was seen in a Baltimore train station. She, like Johnson, vanished into the crowd as a policeman approached her.

Before the year was out, Lafayette Baker and the Potters received several more reports of Booth, Henson, Johnson, and Izola being spotted in several different places along the eastern seaboard.

Baker finally arrived at a decision. He told the Potters that the search for Booth was officially closed. The Potters, however, insisted the assassin was still at large and encouraged Baker to keep searching. According to Andrew Potter, Baker told them that all of the rewards had been paid on Boyd who was dead and buried as Booth, and that the chase was permanently called off.

As time passed, additional evidence accumulated that suggested eventually Booth went to Canada and from there to England. Izola remained in Maryland. In England, Booth allegedly married Elizabeth Burnley, a woman he had known prior to the assassination. It is also believed he changed his name to John Byron Wilkes, a name he once used during his early days as an actor. He remained in England for several years, then traveled to India where, some believe, he died.

Others are convinced the assassin, John Wilkes Booth, returned to the United States.

Chapter XIII

The Return of the Assassin

Almost from the moment the mortally wounded man dressed in Confederate garb was dragged out of Richard Garrett's burning barn on the morning of 26 April 1865, whispers and rumors began circulating that the victim was *not* John Wilkes Booth.

By the time the body reached the Washington Navy Yard, many were saying that the assassin had escaped and that the government was passing off the body of a Confederate spy as that of the actor. A few days later, similar rumors were even spreading throughout Europe and had been picked up and printed by the foreign press.

One of the first to observe that the dying man was not Booth was Wilson D. Kenzie, one of the enlisted troopers with the Sixteenth New York Cavalry present at Garrett's barn. According to author George S. Bryan, Kenzie had known Booth previously when the actor was smuggling medicines to the Confederate troops. Kenzie was not one of the troopers that surrounded the barn but had remained some distance away. After the wounded man was placed on the Garrett porch, a private named Joseph Ziegen ran up to

Kenzie and told him that the officers in charge claimed the man who had been shot was John Wilkes Booth, Lincoln's assassin. Sometime later after "Booth" had been declared dead, Kenzie decided he wanted to get a look at the man who murdered the president. When no one was around, he approached the body, lifted one edge of the blanket that covered it, and stared down at the victim.

During an interview published by the Beloit, Wisconsin, *Daily News* on 20 April 1898, Kenzie stated: "It was not Booth, nor did it resemble him . . . . " He said the corpse he gazed upon had red hair and ruddy features and was wearing a Confederate uniform. Booth, it was well known, had black hair. Confederate Captain James William Boyd had red hair.

On 31 March 1922, Kenzie and trooper Ziegen both signed affidavits stating that the man dragged from Garrett's barn had red hair, was dressed in the uniform of a Confederate officer, and wore heavy, mud-caked, yellow brogans similar to those supplied to Rebel officers. By this time, it was already a matter of record that John Wilkes Booth wore one tall riding boot on his right foot and on his left a shoe provided by Dr. Mudd.

Kenzie told several people at the scene that the dead man was not Booth, but he was told to keep his mouth shut by a Lt. Norris.

Subsequent events, all culminating in the burial of a body in Baltimore's Greenmount Cemetery, provide for considerable doubt that the man who assassinated President Abraham Lincoln had actually been captured and killed. Even a Democratic congressman named Eldridge, a member of an 1867 congressional investigation committee, noted all of the confusion over the body and openly expressed uncertainty about its true identity.

If the corpse that was buried in the Old Arsenal cell was not that of Booth, then who was it? The most compelling evidence to date supports the notion it was James William Boyd.

If that is true, then what eventually became of the assassin John Wilkes Booth?

By the 1930s at least twenty different people had been identified as Booth. Some could easily be dismissed as frauds, impostors, or simply cases of mistaken identity. Others, however, have puzzled investigators and generated considerable reevaluation of the events surrounding the capture and death of John Wilkes Booth.

Some of the more noteworthy cases and sightings are presented here.

In June 1865, a scant two months following the assassination of President Lincoln, two men came aboard the *Mary Porter*, a schooner that was docked in Havana, Cuba. The skipper for the 800-ton ship was Thomas Haggett. During the war, Haggett, using the *Mary Porter*, smuggled contraband through the Union blockades. When his home in New Orleans was burned to the ground by Union troops, Haggett and his wife moved aboard the ship.

Mrs. Haggett, writing in 1898, stated that one of the men who arrived on board the *Mary Porter* was very "haggard and emaciated, suffering under a mental strain as well as from a broken leg . . . ." Haggett told his wife the man was John Wilkes Booth, and that he wanted him to have her cabin for a few days.

Several days later, the *Mary Porter* arrived at Nassau in the Bahamas to deliver a load of sugar. Here, the man who was identified as Booth left the ship, telling Mrs. Haggett he was on his way to England. Before leaving, he presented her with a ring bearing "a large diamond in a gold setting."

In 1898 Mrs. Haggett claimed Booth had died a natural death in England several years earlier.

During the month of August 1866, Lieutenant William M. Tolbert, an officer aboard the Confederate privateer *Shenandoah*, got into an argument with a Southerner in a Calcutta, India, bar. The Southerner claimed he possessed information Booth was alive and well and hiding in Ceylon.

For many years thereafter, Booth was allegedly seen in various parts of the world, sometimes acting in plays, sometimes attending the theater, and sometimes just walking down the street in San Francisco, Rome, Paris, or Vienna.

Most of these reports were undoubtedly false, springing from creative minds. Once in a while, however, a story would come to light that carried with it some level of credibility.

One of these tales came from Andrew Jackson Donelson, once a close companion of John Wilkes Booth. Donelson claimed to have encountered the assassin living on a Pacific Island in the late 1860s.

Donelson, who had served in the army of the Confederacy, was working as first mate on a ship sailing from San Francisco to Shanghai. On arriving at the Palau Islands, some 600 miles east of the Philippines, Donelson, along with several crewmembers, went ashore for water and stores.

During the process of obtaining the needed supplies, Donelson encountered five men and a woman, all Anglos. The leader of the group advanced toward Donelson and extended his hand in greeting. According to Donelson, it was John Wilkes Booth! In an article that appeared in a St. Louis newspaper and quoted by George S. Bryan, Donelson stated "there was no mistaking [Booth's] identity."

The man Donelson claimed was Booth asked the seaman not to tell anyone of his whereabouts for at least a year. Booth introduced the woman as his wife and said that the other four men were not aware of his identity.

Booth told Donelson that his escape had taken him to Mexico, South America, Africa, Turkey, Arabia, Italy, and China. In China, he claimed, he played the title role in *Richard III* before American residents and naval officers.

On the island Booth handed Donelson a gold medal and asked him to deliver it to his brother Edwin. The same medal, according to Bryan, had once been awarded to Edwin Booth by "the citizens of New York."

In 1870 a stranger arrived in the tiny town of Forestville, located in northern California's Sonoma County, about fifty miles northwest of San Francisco. In this part of California, a number of Southern secessionists found refuge. The stranger gave his name as Thomas Jerome, but in a short time many residents came to believe he was John Wilkes Booth.

According to one story, a Secret Service officer arrived in Forestville seeking to interrogate Jerome. On learning this information, Jerome fled from the region, returning only when the operative returned to Washington.

Jerome bore a remarkable resemblance to Booth, and when Forestville residents were shown pictures of Booth, they identified the images as Jerome. Jerome, himself, never claimed to be Booth, and a handwriting analysis failed to link him to the actor. One subsequent investigation reported that Jerome's real name was Thomas McGittigan and that he had originally come from Philadelphia.

During the early 1880s, an Episcopal minister going by the name of James G. Armstrong lived in Richmond,

Virginia. Armstrong looked remarkably like John Wilkes Booth, loved the theater and attended often, and manifested a skilled dramatic technique during his sermons.

Armstrong walked with a cane as a result of a limp; his left leg, he once said, had been broken in a fall. Armstrong also had a scar on the back of his neck, a scar corresponding to the one mentioned by Dr. May during the inquest of the body aboard the *Montauk*.

Armstrong was once called into court to testify in a lawsuit against the church. During the questioning, an attorney for the plaintiff asked him point blank if he was John Wilkes Booth. Armstrong did not deny the association, merely replying, "I am on trial as James Armstrong, not as John Wilkes Booth."

In 1884 Armstrong left Richmond for Atlanta. In 1888 he resigned his post with the church and became a paid lecturer. His favorite topics, according to researcher Bryan, were *Hamlet* and *Richard III*. During this time, it is reported, he confessed to his wife that he was, in fact, John Wilkes Booth.

In the late 1880s, Edwin Booth was performing in an Atlanta theater and Armstrong was in the audience. During the play, the elder Booth chanced to look upon the features of Armstrong and, startled, suddenly paused in his monologue. At 1:00 A.M. the following morning, Edwin Booth was transported by carriage to Armstrong's home where he visited with him for several hours. What the two men discussed was never revealed.

On another occasion, an Atlanta hotel guest was gazing out the window of the dining room when Armstrong passed by on the sidewalk outside. The guest, visibly disturbed, pointed at Armstrong and told diners at a nearby table that the man who just walked by was John Wilkes Booth. When they informed him it was the Reverend James

G. Armstrong, the guest replied, "That may be the name he goes by here, but his real name is John Wilkes Booth!"

Armstrong died in 1891. Because of persistent rumors that he might have been Booth, the New York *Herald* undertook an investigation in 1903 into the mysterious minister's past. The *Herald* concluded that Armstrong could not have been Booth, claiming it discovered evidence the minister was living in western Ohio during the time the actor was known to be residing in New York and Baltimore.

A rather provocative case of a man believed by some to be John Wilkes Booth involved a resident of Morgan County, Tennessee, from 1866 to 1885.

One day a stranger who gave his name as Sinclair arrived in Wartburg, about forty miles west of Knoxville. He checked into the hotel where he remained for many weeks. Sinclair stayed to himself, preferring to remain in his locked room for days at a time.

During one of his few strolls through town, Sinclair accidentally lost a small portfolio. It was found later and contained a handwritten account providing intimate details of the assassination of Abraham Lincoln, details that would have been known only to one who had participated.

During his stay at the hotel, Sinclair fell quite ill and had to be attended by a physician. While suffering from a period of high fever, Sinclair, according to the doctor, screamed out the names Atzerodt, Herold, Paine, Mudd, and Spangler. Before his fever broke, he also told the doctor that his real name was not Sinclair but Booth.

Sinclair resided in Wharton for almost twenty years. In 1885 a visitor to the town, after descending from a carriage, spotted Sinclair walking along a sidewalk. The stranger walked up to him, extended his hand, and said, "Hello, Booth."

Sinclair, turned and hurried away, and was never seen again after that day.

During the time ex-soldier, statesman, and lawyer General Albert Pike resided in Washington, D.C., he became a fan of the theater and attended numerous performances. One of his favorite actors was reputed to have been John Wilkes Booth.

One evening in 1885 in Fort Worth, Texas, Pike was drinking with old friend and newspaperman Col. M.W. Connolly in the barroom of the Pickwick Hotel. As the two men conversed, Pike's gaze wandered to the mirror behind the bar. There he saw the image of a man he recognized immediately. Turning, Pike stared directly at a customer seated a few tables away. Clearly startled, Pike is reported to have exclaimed, "My God, it's John Wilkes Booth!"

With that, the man at the table jumped up and ran out of the bar.

Blanche de Bar Booth, daughter of Junius Brutus Booth and niece of John Wilkes, told of what may have been a near encounter with her famous uncle.

During a 1902 visit to Enid, Oklahoma, Blanche Booth responded to a knock on her hotel door. Without opening it, she asked who was there. The voice on the other side said, "Blanche, don't you want to see Johnnie?" Members of the Booth family always called John Wilkes "Johnnie." Believing a joke was being played on her by some actor friend, she said she did not wish to be disturbed. The voice on the other side said he would call later, and then a card was slipped under the door. The name on the card was "John Wilkes Booth."

Several years following the events at the Garrett farm, Edwin Booth, accompanied by his mother, was in England for a series of performances. Following a play one evening, Edwin and Mrs. Booth were driving away from the theater when the mother, looking out of the carriage window, spotted a man across the street and screamed, "Johnnie! There goes Johnnie!" Edwin had to hold on to her to keep her from leaping out of the vehicle.

While struggling to calm down his mother, Edwin looked out the window, saw the man, and was heard to exclaim, "My God! It *is* Johnnie!"

Edwin left the carriage and pursued the man, overtaking him some distance away from the carriage. He spent several minutes conversing with him but never revealed the substance of the discussion.

One of the most highly publicized and perplexing accounts relative to the return of John Wilkes Booth involves a man known at different times as John St. Helen and David E. George.

In his book *The Escape and Suicide of John Wilkes Booth*, author Finis L. Bates writes of meeting St. Helen in Granbury, Texas, a quiet little town some forty miles southwest of Fort Worth. Bates was a young lawyer who had recently opened an office in the small town. St. Helen dropped by one day and asked Bates to defend him against a charge of running a saloon without a license in the nearby town of Glen Rose. St. Helen admitted to Bates he was, indeed, guilty of the charge, but stated he would resist appearing at a Federal Court hearing in Tyler. The barkeeper told Bates his real name was not John St. Helen and that he was concerned that his true identity might be discovered. The risk, he said, was too great.

Several weeks later, St. Helen moved to Granbury. In his book, Bates described St. Helen as having "more money than was warranted by his stock in trade." According to Bates' notes, St. Helen had "penetrating black eyes" that manifested "desperation and a capacity for crime." He also said St. Helen showed an "intimacy with every detail of theatrical work," and often kept theater-related periodicals in his room. St. Helen could recite most of Shakespeare's plays, and was particularly fond of *Richard III*. Townspeople remembered St. Helen as "vain."

Late one night in 1877, Bates was summoned to St. Helen's bedside. He was seriously ill, he said, and confided in Bates that he did not think he would live. St. Helen told Bates to search under his pillow where he would find a tintype. Bates searched for and retrieved it, a tintype that bore the image of John St. Helen.

St. Helen told the lawyer, if he should die, to please send the picture to Edwin Booth in Baltimore with a note stating that the man in the picture had finally passed away. St. Helen then placed a hand on Bates' forearm, drew him closer, and told him he was John Wilkes Booth, the assassin of President Abraham Lincoln!

The stunned Bates promised he would, if necessary, send the picture to Edwin Booth. He sat up with the sick St. Helen all night.

St. Helen remained seriously ill for several weeks but finally began improving. When he was able, he invited Bates to walk with him some distance out of town. During the walk, St. Helen once again told the lawyer that he was John Wilkes Booth, and he pleaded with Bates to keep the knowledge secret.

According to St. Helen, Andrew Johnson was the principal instigator of the assassination of President Abraham Lincoln. St. Helen related that he (as Booth) did, in fact, visit with Johnson on the afternoon of 14 April only hours before the assassination, and that the vice president informed him that it had been arranged for General Grant to be out of town and that the way had been cleared to allow the assassin to escape into Maryland.

For his part, Bates respected the confidentiality of St. Helen's admission, though he was initially disbelieving. Throughout their conversation, St. Helen related a number of other details relative to the murder of Lincoln, the subsequent escape from Ford's Theater, and the flight through the Maryland and Virginia countryside.

Some of St. Helens' descriptions and information, as told to Bates, have been questioned by researchers. Others, however, maintain they could only have come from some intimate experience with the assassination events, particularly those associated with the Garrett farm. How, then, could St. Helen be aware of Booth's movements and other aspects of the escape that were virtually unknown to historians? If St. Helen were merely an impostor, one must wonder why he did not relate commonly known and well-publicized aspects of the assassination. Instead, he provided versions somewhat different from the accepted ones, versions that, on investigation, bear some level of credibility.

One particularly telling piece of information related to the diary. Most historians claim Booth's diary was taken from the pockets of the dying man at Garrett's farm. According to journals and papers analyzed by researchers Balsiger and Sellier, however, Booth's diary was lost in a grove of trees where he camped with Henson near Gambo Creek after escaping into Virginia. St. Helen told that, on 22 April, he had "discovered that he had lost his diary, some letters, and a picture of my sister" by the time he reached Port Royal on the Rappahannock River.

St. Helen also told Bates that on 24 April, he fled westward through West Virginia and Kentucky, eventually making his way to Mississippi and thence to Indian Territory. After spending some time in the American West, St. Helen went into Mexico where he disguised himself as a priest. From Mexico he traveled to California in 1866 or 1867 where he said he met with his mother and his older brother Junius in San Francisco.

St. Helen arrived in Texas after spending a year in New Orleans where he went by the name of Ney and taught school there. He eventually settled in Glen Rose where he assumed the name John St. Helen and operated a saloon. In October of 1872, he moved to Granbury.

A few months following St. Helen's revelations, lawyer Bates moved to Memphis, Tennessee, where he established what eventually became a successful law practice. In his spare time, he began reading everything he could find on the assassination of Abraham Lincoln. The more he studied the subject, the more he grew convinced that John St. Helen was actually John Wilkes Booth.

In January 1898 Bates wrote to the Secretary of War Alger, explained that he possessed evidence that Booth was still alive, and inquired if such information was important to the War Department.

The War Department replied it was not.

On 13 January 1903 the body of a man named David E. George was transported from his room at the Grand Avenue Hotel in Enid, Oklahoma, to the undertaking establishment of W.B. Penniman. George, known around town as a handyman and house painter, had committed suicide the previous night. George was also known by Enid residents to be an alcoholic and perhaps even a drug addict since he regularly took morphine. He died from a strong dose of strychnine.

While Penniman's assistant, W.H. Ryan, was embalming the body, Reverend E.C. Harper walked in. Harper was a Methodist preacher who had just completed a funeral service in the outer room. Harper glanced down at the body of George and cried out, "Do you know who that is?"

When assistant Ryan said he did not, Reverend Harper explained that the body belonged to none other than John Wilkes Booth, the assassin of President Abraham Lincoln. He told Ryan that "George" had confessed his identity to Mrs. Harper three years earlier. Mrs. Harper subsequently made a statement wherein she confirmed she had gone to the funeral parlor on 15 January and identified the corpse of David E. George as the man who admitted to her in El Reno, Oklahoma, in 1900 that he was John Wilkes Booth.

During the next few days, newspapers around the country carried the story that a man believed by some to be John Wilkes Booth had died in Enid, Oklahoma. In Memphis, Finis Bates read the article and wondered if the dead man named David E. George might be the man he once knew as John St. Helen.

Bates departed Memphis and arrived in Enid on 23 January. On the following morning he went to view the body. From a folder he withdrew the tintype of John St. Helen and held it up next to the face of the corpse.

It was, according to Bates, the same man.

For several days the body remained on display at Penniman's establishment. Because it went unclaimed, it was eventually placed in a back room where it was stored for years. Finally, Finis Bates came forward and claimed the body.

It was subsequently learned by Bates that George had worked as a house painter in El Reno, Oklahoma. When he wasn't working, which was most of the time, he just hung around a few retail establishments and occasionally the police station. Bates also discovered that George regularly received large amounts of money from mysterious sources. The lawyer was convinced that George, like St. Helen, was getting money from the Booth family. Bates learned that, at his death, George was worth approximately $30,000 and carried a $5,000 life insurance policy. When George left El Reno for Enid, however, he owed money to several people.

In April 1900 George, in a fit of depression, had swallowed a large amount of prescription drugs and sincerely believed he was going to die. While still barely conscious, he told a Miss Young, who was to become the wife of the Reverend E.C. Harper the following year, that he had a confession to make. He told her that he had killed "one of the best men who ever lived, Abraham Lincoln." He asked the woman to bring him a pen and paper and when she did he scribbled, "I am going to die before the sun goes down." He signed it "J. Wilkes Booth."

George recovered from this suicide attempt and several weeks later moved from El Reno to Enid, about 65 miles to the north. On the morning of 13 January 1903 while staying at Enid's Grand Avenue Hotel, George swallowed a large amount of strychnine and died a short time later.

Were St. Helen and George the same man? And were they John Wilkes Booth? It may never be known.

Some critical researchers, Bryan foremost among them, contend Bates worked hard to make the two men appear to be the same, and in so doing purposely altered some of the facts. In spite of Bryan's contentions, St. Helen and George shared many of the same characteristics: They drank heavily; they were inclined to be loud and boisterous on occasion; they were known to launch into extended soliloquies and poetry; both carried a gun. Both men were apparently well educated, and both were intimate with the theater and with Shakespeare. While living in El Reno, George was remembered as having participated in a number of amateur productions and providing excellent performances.

Both St. Helen and George dressed in the manner of Booth. Bates noted that both men always wore "a black semi-dress suit style, of the best fabrics, always with the turndown Byron collar and dark tie . . . tailor made, new and well pressed, his pants well creased, his shoes new patent leather and his hat a new black Stetson derby."

George possessed certain physical characteristics that were similar to those of Booth. The only officially recognized comparison study of the day, the Bertillion Examination, evaluated the features of both David E. George and John Wilkes Booth and found some disturbing similarities. The shape of George's head, specifically the structure of the forehead, as well as the contour of the face around the eyes and the jaw line, bear a striking resemblance to Booth. The Bertillion analysis also revealed that the structure of the nose, particularly the bridge of the nose, the "indenture of [George's] left nostril, and the distance from nose to mouth bear some resemblance to Booth's." Other features described by the analysis included a cocked right eyebrow manifested by both men, the ears, and the striking similarity of their hands.

Many skeptics state the eyes of David E. George were enough to dismiss the claim that he was Booth. George's eyes, as described by the mortician, were blue-gray. According to a number of government documents, Booth's eyes were black. Asia Booth, the actor's own sister, wrote they were hazel.

George, according to Bates, bore the marks of a broken right leg, not the left that Booth broke at the end of his leap at Ford's Theater. Others who claimed to have examined the corpse stated they found no evidence of a break at all.

George's signature as "J. Wilkes Booth," according to some analysts, bore little resemblance to Booth's actual handwriting. Others, however, maintain there were certain critical similarities.

A Dr. Clarence True Wilson told a writer in 1932 that he had conducted a thorough study of the George-Booth similarities and was convinced they were one and the same. Wilson was also quoted as stating he learned that the name of the man who died in Garrett's barn was Boyd and that John Wilkes Booth lived long afterward only to finally die in Enid. Wilson claimed he was in possession of the George mummy for three years, during which time he studied it extensively.

Bates showed photographs of St. Helen and George to a number of people who had known Booth. The city editor of the El Reno newspaper was a man named Brown who had lived in Washington, D.C., Baltimore, and New York during the 1860s, regularly attended the theater, and saw Booth perform many times. On being shown photographs of George, Brown stated, "I never saw David E. George, but these are pictures of John Wilkes Booth."

Brown, who was serving in the army during the time of the assassination, was in Washington during the time the body of the man killed at Garrett's arrived on the *Montauk*. He told Bates that "... there was a belief, quite general among members of the Federal army with whom I came in contact, that the body... was not that of John Wilkes Booth."

Bates showed photographs of Booth to L. Threadkell, who once employed John St. Helen as a teamster in 1867. Threadkell unhesitatingly identified the images of Booth as St. Helen.

Bates also showed the tintype of St. Helen and photographs of George to Joseph Jefferson in April 1903. Jefferson had known Booth since childhood, was a fellow actor, and performed in many of the same plays with him. After examining the images closely, Jefferson looked up at Bates and said, “This is John Wilkes Booth.”

One particularly compelling piece of evidence is related to Booth’s signet ring, a piece of jewelry he was seldom without. It will be remembered that the ring was not found on the body of the man killed at Garrett’s barn.

David E. George wore a similar ring. Some time before expiring from his dose of strychnine, George told a neighbor that, on spotting two law enforcement officers approaching him, he feared he would be identified. He pulled the ring from his finger and swallowed it.

The mummy of David E. George was examined by a group of seven physicians at Chicago’s Northwestern University in December 1931. The group was headed by Dr. Otto L. Schmidt, once president of the prestigious Chicago Historical Society. Another member of the group was Dr. Lewis L. McArthur, one of the country’s leading X-ray specialists at the time.

The George mummy was subjected to X-rays and dissection. During the examination, according to their report, the team found evidence of a broken leg, although it was not stated whether it was the right or left.

The most astounding discovery, however, was that of a ring embedded slightly in the flesh of the body cavity. Though the surface had been modified somewhat as a result of the action of digestive juices, it was believed the initials “JWB” could be discerned on its face. Dr. Schmidt subsequently wrote: “I can say safely that we believe Booth’s body is here in my office.”

Others maintain there was nothing in the personalities of either St. Helen or George to suggest they could have been John Wilkes Booth. Booth was regarded by most as being "handsome, vital, magnetic, brilliant" and possessed about him "a restless, irresistible energy, something dynamic which attracted people to him, and won their liking." According to writer Izola Forrester, there was "no such compelling quality about either [St. Helen or George]." The two, she states, were "ordinary, commonplace . . . without distinction or education, and without a trace of Booth's mannerisms or artistic ability."

The evidence for St. Helen being George and for either or both of those men being Booth remains intriguing and provocative, yet thus far inconclusive.

Given the available facts, however, a number of researchers are convinced that David E. George was the assassin John Wilkes Booth. Most of those discrediting the George mummy as being that of Booth have been journalists, and, as author Roscoe says, journalists are not professional detectives.

The fate of the David E. George mummy presents yet another mystery. At one point, Bates offered to sell the mummy to *The Dearborn Independent* for $1,000. Another time he offered it to Henry Ford for $100,000. Both declined to purchase it. During the 1920s and 1930s, Bates leased or sold the mummified corpse of David E. George to a carnival promoter who charged patrons twenty-five cents to view "The Assassin of President Abraham Lincoln." The body was still being displayed during the 1940s. After that, the promoter went bankrupt and moved to Declo, Idaho, where he placed the mummy in a chair on his front porch and charged neighbors ten cents to see it. The mummy eventually disappeared, and to this day no one is certain of its whereabouts. It is reputed to exist in a private collection somewhere.

In 1990 three research pathologists at the Regional Forensic Center in Memphis, Tennessee, undertook a search for the so-called Booth mummy. They were convinced David E. George was John Wilkes Booth and believed they could prove it. To date, the mummy has not been found.

Another "Booth" showed up in Sewanee, Tennessee. He lived and worked there as a cabinetmaker and actually went by the name of John W. Booth. When questioned about his name, the cabinetmaker only replied that he was a distant cousin of the famous assassin. The Sewanee Booth had wavy black hair, a black moustache, dark eyes, weighed approximately 145 pounds, and was described by some of the Sewanee residents as a man who knew quite a bit about the theater.

On 25 February 1872 the Sewanee Booth married Louisa Payne, the daughter of a Presbyterian minister. During the evening following the ceremony, the Sewanee Booth pointed to a scar on one of his legs and told his wife it was the result of a break he suffered during a fall on the stage at Ford's Theater when he killed President Lincoln. He went on to tell her that he would soon receive some $100,000 from the group that was responsible for the assassination of Lincoln.

On 1 July 1872 the Sewanee Booth, his wife, and her son from a previous marriage moved to Memphis where Booth took a job in a cottonseed mill. On two occasions, a group of men were spotted stalking the Sewanee Booth. When he found out about it, he moved his family to new quarters.

One evening Booth did not return home from his job. When his wife went to the mill, she was told that two men arrived, exchanged what appeared to be secret signs with her husband, and the three left together.

The Sewanee John W. Booth was never seen again. A few months later, Louisa Booth gave birth to a daughter, Laura Ida Booth.

Following the death of David E. George, Enid officials began receiving letters from Laura Ida Booth, who claimed George was her father. Subsequent investigation, however, concluded the Sewanee John W. Booth could not have been David E. George.

The Louisa Payne Booth claim is not particularly convincing. On the other hand, the discovery of another woman, who many contend is the daughter of John Wilkes Booth, deserves some considered attention.

During the 1890s, Ogarita Booth Henderson had often been identified and referred to as the daughter of John Wilkes Booth, a charge she emphatically denied in public.

Henderson was active in the theater and was occasionally seen wearing a brooch containing a small portrait of John Wilkes Booth. Several who knew Booth stated that Henderson possessed the same features, hair, eyes, and high brow of the assassin.

In 1937 a book titled *This One Mad Act* was published and purported to tell the true story of John Wilkes Booth and his secret family. The author was listed as Izola Laura Forrester, purportedly the daughter of Ogarita Henderson and granddaughter of John Wilkes Booth. Author George S. Bryan was highly critical of *This One Mad Act* and claimed Izola Forrester was actually a woman named Mann Page, who once worked as a staff writer for newspapers. The truth is Mann Page was, in fact, a *nom de plume* for Forrester, and while her inexperience as a researcher of history shows up from time to time in the book, her contentions are equally, if not more, compelling than those of Bryan.

In the book, Forrester writes that her grandmother, Izola Mills D'Arcy, met John Wilkes Booth in Richmond where the actor was appearing with a stock company. Others contend they met while both were involved with smuggling quinine to Confederate hospitals. Not long afterward, Forrester contends, Booth and D'Arcy were married in Cos Cob, Connecticut, on 9 January 1859. The ceremony was conducted by the Reverend Peleg Weaver in his home. The marriage was recorded in the church log and shown to a member of the Forrester family during the early 1900s.

The newlyweds decided to keep the marriage secret, a decision that has confused some researchers. The fact is, actors and actresses of the day often posed as single before the public simply because it was good for business. Booth's own father, Junius Brutus Booth Sr., married his first wife at twenty years of age and kept her, along with the birth of two children, a secret from the theatergoing public for many years. They were left in England.

After the marriage to Izola, John continued acting, mostly in Richmond, and his wife continued to live in the Shenandoah Valley. On 23 October 1859, Ogarita, the mother of author Forrester, was born to John and Izola.

Ogarita grew to be a noted stage performer who initially used the name Ogarita Wilkes, and later, Rita Booth. Ogarita died in Binghampton, New York, on 12 April 1892. An obituary that appeared in the *New York World* on 15 April, noted that she was the daughter of John Wilkes Booth and stated that several people "who knew Booth . . . noted in her the clear-cut features . . . the curly hair and high brow" of the actor.

It was also pointed out in *This One Mad Act* that the mother of Henry Johnson, Booth's valet who played an important role in his escape, worked for Izola D'Arcy at one time.

Following the assassination, Izola changed her name, moved to Baltimore, and lived with John H. Stevenson, a longtime friend of John Wilkes Booth. They eventually married in 1870. For most of her life she lived in fear that her children, going through life with the name Booth, would be scorned. Izola remained in contact with the Booth family, particularly John's sister Rosalie, who apparently provided the family with money. Izola and her two children also were friends with John Matthews, a friend of the family and fellow actor.

During the autumn of 1868, according to Forrester, Izola D'Arcy Booth, in the company of John H. Stevenson, traveled to California to meet with her husband in San Diego. She remained for several months. After spending time with Booth, she returned to Baltimore where she eventually gave birth to her son, Harry Jerome, on 27 February 1870. Some researchers are convinced that the woman introduced as Booth's wife to Andrew Jackson Donelson on the Palau Islands in the late 1860s was actually Izola D'Arcy.

As a youth, Harry bore what Forrester referred to as "a striking resemblance" to Booth. When Harry was a young man, he was told by John H. Stevenson just a few days before his death that he was not his son, that he was the son of John Wilkes Booth.

In 1894 Harry was the featured entertainment at a banquet. Seated in the audience was the guest of a family member. Following Harry's performance, the stranger walked up to him and, with tears in his eyes, embraced the young man.

"Don't you remember me, Mr. Booth?" he asked.

The stunned Harry grew white with anger and asked why he was addressed in such a manner. The stranger, according to Izola Forrester, said, "Because that is your name, sir." He went on to introduce himself as George Whyte Smith and explained he had been in the employ of the Booth family years ago, eventually moving on to work with John Wilkes' sister, Rosalie. Whyte went on to say that he recalled a young Harry visiting Rosalie's house with his mother, Ogarita, and that Whyte used to hold him on his lap and feed him cake.

Harry died in 1918.

Author Forester also wrote of a man named Colonel John Young who claimed he received a number of letters during the 1890s from a man who signed them "John Wilkes." John Wilkes lived in Bombay, India, and the letters arrived from that city as well as from Calcutta, Shanghai, and the island of Ceylon. Young claimed he became friends with John Wilkes during an Asian journey in 1871 and the two maintained a correspondence. While spending time with his new friend, Young met "a Negro named Henry," who accompanied John Wilkes in his travels.

Young also recalled the account of a man named James Kelly, a former actor who stayed in touch with many theatrical performers. Kelly met Booth in 1858, even acted with him as a member of the same stock company. Kelly also knew Booth's valet Henry Johnson.

During the 1870s, Kelly traveled to New York City on business from his home in Grand Rapids, Michigan. While strolling down Broadway Avenue, Kelly encountered Henry Johnson and spoke to him. Johnson appeared nervous and tried to get away. During the conversation, Kelly asked Henry what he was doing, and the black man replied that he had been working for Edwin Booth "ever since Master John got away." Under rigorous questioning, Kelly got from

Henry the story that Booth, accompanied by Henry, eventually sailed to Liverpool, England, where they remained for a short time, and thence on to Bombay.

Persisting, Kelly said he obtained Booth's Bombay address from the valet and wrote his old friend a letter. To his utter surprise, he received a return letter from "John Wilkes." According to Kelly, the handwriting on the letter was identical to Booth's signatures on some old theater posters he possessed. Booth, as a young man, often acted under the name "John B. Wilkes." Col. Young stated that he was convinced Edwin Booth was entirely aware that his brother was alive and living in Bombay.

In 1926 Izola Forrester discovered another piece of compelling evidence that John Wilkes Booth survived. It will be recalled that, during his frantic ride through the streets of Washington following the assassination, Booth encountered his friend Billy Andrews who, after examining the actor's broken leg, bound it with his silk cravat and scarf pin. Andrews, like many others who had known Booth, had been jailed for a time as a conspirator but eventually released. Years later, he moved to New York where he dabbled in politics and became a special counsel for the president of the Erie Railway.

One evening, Andrews told a number of assembled friends about his encounter with Booth on the streets of Washington on that night of 14 April 1865. What stunned the assembled guests, however, was when Andrew admitted that, four years later, the pin had been returned to him—by Izola D'Arcy Booth!

In 1932 author Forrester located and visited with Harry Jerome Stevenson's ex-wife. During the interview, the former Mrs. Harry Stevenson, now Mrs. Godfrey, told Izola that she had known all along that Harry was the son of John

Wilkes Booth and that he was born five years following the assassin's escape.

In 1882 Izola Booth Stevenson moved to Connecticut and the town of Canterbury where she somehow managed to live well. Though no one knew for certain from where her fortune came, it was often suggested she received support from the Booth family. Throughout her life, she never spoke of John Wilkes Booth or of the death of Abraham Lincoln. She did, however, wear a medallion around her neck that contained a photograph of the actor. In addition, several photographs of Booth hung on the walls of her home.

As a child, Izola Forrester played with her grandmother's collection of seashells. Years later when the shells were examined, it was discovered they came from a species known to exist only in the Palau Islands in the Pacific Ocean.

Forrester died on 9 November 1887. Her search for the truth about her grandfather has added to the growing evidence that John Wilkes Booth, the assassin of Abraham Lincoln, escaped and returned.

Chapter XIV

Analysis

To those researchers who have studied the Lincoln assassination and the flight of John Wilkes Booth in depth, a number of somewhat disturbing elements are apparent.

Following the actual killing of the president, numerous aspects of the assassin's escape are well documented, but others are sketchy, inferred, and subject to a wide variety of interpretations.

Far too much of the official record as it relates to the events at Garrett's barn, the body, and the burial are suspect, confusing, and more often than not contradictory. The more one studies the existing materials, the more one comes away convinced of ineptitude, cover-up, and conspiracy on the part of government officials responsible for handling the Booth situation.

Another problem relates to official documents. Scholarship oriented toward the plight of John Wilkes Booth was officially stifled for seventy years. The War Department kept the official files of the so-called assassination conspiracy, along with those associated with the pursuit and capture of Booth, under lock and key for seven decades.

Some have suggested hiding the documents was done in order to protect government officials from implication in Lincoln's assassination and Booth's escape. Researcher Roscoe hints the military censorship was intended to "conceal the survival of John Wilkes Booth."

Still others have maintained the secrecy was intended to keep the public from finding out about massive incompetence. During the time the materials were locked up, it is suspected many important documents were removed.

To add to the confusion, most traditional writers of Booth history and the Lincoln era have essentially perpetuated the government's version of events by using government data, government documents, and government-approved transcriptions as gospel. Far too much of the existing "history" is little more than repetition of material quoted from the works of earlier writers.

Author William Hanchett blames professional historians for writing some truly bad books about the Lincoln assassination, and he further states that "professional historians allowed the assassination to fall through the gaps separating the two traditional fields of historical scholarship—the Civil War and Reconstruction. It [Booth and Lincoln] did not seem to belong to one or the other." As a result, most of what Americans know about John Wilkes Booth, or more precisely, what they think they know, is simply not true.

As new documents, journals, diaries, and papers are discovered and become available, they do little to support the traditional, that is, government, position on the events related to the Lincoln assassination. The truth is, they accomplish quite the opposite—the more that is learned about this special period in American history, the more it becomes likely, if not apparent, that Booth was never captured and killed by the authorities, but escaped from their clutches to live for at least another two decades, possibly more.

Ultimately, what the researcher is faced with is an incredible amount of contradiction and doubt regarding the veracity of the traditional and "accepted" version of the escape, capture, and killing of John Wilkes Booth.

What, then, is the truth?

For purposes of analysis and summary, critical and conflicting aspects of Booth's escape are herein considered. They include the specific differences between David Herold and Ed Henson, the body of the man who was shot and killed at Garrett's barn, the disposal of the body by the federal government, the subsequent reburial of the body at Baltimore's Greenmount Cemetery, Edwin Booth's role, and the "return" of the assassin John Wilkes Booth.

Herold vs. Henson

History generally records that Booth, in the company of David Herold, fled across parts of Maryland and Virginia until meeting his fate at the Garrett farm on the morning of 26 April 1865.

Given a thorough evaluation of the traditional history, along with the relatively recent discovery of new evidence, historians would be well served to reexamine the so-called facts regarding these two men and their respective roles.

The introduction of the mysterious Ed Henson into the activities of the last few days of John Wilkes Booth is, in part, the result of the work of researchers Balsiger and Sellier, who claim to have uncovered pertinent evidence in the form of the Andrew Potter papers. While the authenticity of the documents examined by these two researchers may be questionable, the materials and their subsequent interpretation have forced serious, unbiased scholars to reconsider some aspects of the man who accompanied Booth.

At least five pertinent factors must be considered in a comparison analysis of these two important figures: appearance, logistics, identification by others, personality and behavior, and the isolation of David Herold by the government following his capture.

Appearance

According to the documents, the two men—Herold and Henson—were quite similar in appearance. Henson was somewhat older, but if the photograph of this enigmatic character in the possession of Indiana State University scholar Ray A. Neff is authentic, it is easy to see how the two men could be confused with one another.

Henson was allegedly involved in smuggling supplies and medicines to the Southern army along with Booth. He eventually settled in Washington, D.C. and had occasional contact with Booth. David Herold likewise was often found in the company of John Wilkes Booth—running errands, fetching, and essentially serving at the actor's beck and call.

There exists, then, the possibility that one could have been mistaken for the other.

Logistics

According to the research of Balsiger and Sellier, Herold crossed from the capital to Maryland on the afternoon of 14 April in the company of another and was miles away at the time of the assassination and Booth's escape. Henson, on the other hand, allegedly crossed the bridge only minutes after Booth and joined him at Good Hope Hill. Unfortunately, neither of these events can be proven beyond a shadow of a doubt. Despite this lack of proof, however, there exists some compelling evidence that suggests Herold had been arrested by the National Detective Police on 16 April and was already in custody *at the time of the initial pursuit of Booth*.

Considered by itself, this information does not carry much weight. Considered in light of other evidence, particularly the problems associated with the identification of Herold, along with Herold's own testimony, it takes on significant proportions.

Identification

The *only* basis on which a determination was made that David Herold was the man who crossed the Navy Yard Bridge minutes after Booth is the testimony of Nailor's Stable (Livery) employee John Fletcher.

When Navy Yard Bridge guard Silas Cobb was called on to identify Herold as that man, he was clearly uncertain, stating Herold was somewhat taller and had a darker complexion. There exists no solid evidence on which to base the contention that David Herold crossed the Navy Yard Bridge behind Booth.

The identification provided by Dr. Samuel Mudd likewise does nothing to convince anyone that it was Herold who accompanied Booth to the physician's house near Bryantown on the morning of 15 April 1865. During his interrogation by authorities, Mudd was shown a photograph of Herold and asked if it was the man who accompanied Booth. Mudd replied, " . . . I do not recognize it as that of this young man . . . I asked his name. He gave it as Henston [sic] . . . . " In other words, within only a few days following the visit to Mudd's house, the doctor did not recognize David Herold as the man who accompanied Booth.

Personality and Behavior

Perhaps the most telling differences between Herold and Henson are associated with their respective personality and behavior.

Since Ed Henson was an accomplished smuggler, it is not unreasonable to assume he possessed a respectable level of self-confidence, maturity, and composure. He likely had a keenly developed sense of adventure, since he so readily agreed to accompany Booth on his flight.

According to testimony, the man with Booth dealt expeditiously with Surratt Tavern proprietor John Lloyd. At Dr. Mudd's home, he quickly and confidently assumed a number of responsibilities including taking the initiative to approach the house, make introductions, ask directions, converse with Mudd, and aid the ailing Booth.

On arriving at the farm of Samuel Cox, Booth's companion consulted with the guide, Oscar (also known as Oswald) Swann, paid him twelve dollars, and warned him that if he mentioned the incident he would be killed. While hiding in the pine thicket near Cox's farm, he took charge, acted maturely and responsibly, constructed a lean-to, and removed the horses from the premises so they would not give away the hiding place to passing cavalrymen.

The tricky crossing of the Potomac River was clearly handled by a man experienced with such things, a man not inclined to panic during an emergency.

Such behavior and competence was not evident in David Herold. Herald was characterized by several different witnesses as "doltish," "trifling," "a mere boy," and "slightly retarded." During the Conspiracy Trial, soldier Willie Jett described Herold as "not . . . very self-possessed, his voice trembled very much, and he was a good deal agitated." The Herold family physician said Herold was "very lightly trivial, unreliable . . . with . . . the mind of an eleven-year-old child." These characteristics do not in any way represent the personality and behavior of the man who accompanied Booth through the trials and agonies during the flight through the Maryland and Virginia countryside.

The competence and poise manifested by the man who was with Booth at Surratt's Tavern, Dr. Mudd's residence, the Cox farm, and crossing the Potomac River was not at all evident in the reactions of the terror-stricken young man who was captured at Garrett's barn.

There are so many clear and obvious differences between David Herold and the man who rode with Booth that it is rather surprising this was not picked up by earlier researchers. A thorough and logical analysis of these events forces one to conclude that Herold and Booth's companion were two different men.

Two other factors should concern the serious Booth scholar as it relates to David Herold. First of all, why was there such a rush to try, convict, and hang Herold and the other conspirators? Secondly, why was Herold not permitted to testify or talk to anyone during the time he was in custody?

Given the available evidence, the only logical conclusion is that the man who accompanied John Wilkes Booth during his escape into Maryland and Virginia was *not* David Herold. The only other possibility is Ed Henson.

What became of Ed Henson following the escape? The Potter papers, as interpreted by Balsiger and Sellier, suggest Henson traveled with Booth and Henry Johnson to Europe, later returned to Fort Wayne, Indiana, where he changed his name to Edwin Henderson, married, and lived out the remainder of his life as a farmer.

The Body

The Man in the Barn

The body taken from the Garrett farm and placed on board the *Montauk* had little in common with John Wilkes Booth.

Though John Wilkes Booth and James William Boyd shared several similarities, the obvious differences between the two men are numerous, clear, and convincing.

With regard to similarities, both had comparable facial features, both had the same initials, both had their initials tattooed on some part of their body, both were approximately the same height and weight, both were Southern sympathizers, and both had an injured leg.

While these half-dozen similarities might seem remarkable, the differences were so striking that it begs enormous indulgence on the part of the researcher to remotely consider that the man killed at Garrett's barn and delivered to the government vessel *Montauk* and John Wilkes Booth were the same.

Following is a summary of the most striking differences:

1. The man killed at Garrett's barn had what was described as a "long, scraggly" mustache. Booth shaved his off eleven days earlier, and ferryman William Rollins, who saw Booth only two days prior to the event at Garrett's farm, stated *he had no mustache*. Given the laws governing endocrinology, it takes considerably more than two days to grow a long scraggly mustache.

2. The man at Garrett's had red hair. Booth's hair was jet-black.

3. Booth was twenty-six years old. The body at Garrett's belonged to a man clearly older. James William Boyd was forty-three years old.

4. The body that lay upon the deck of the *Montauk* was described as "thin," "gaunt," and "starved." Marshal John L. Smith, who had seen Booth only a few days prior to the assassination, said he "looked well and as fleshy as I ever saw him." According to Thomas Jones, Booth had been fed well during his stay at the pine thicket near Cox's farm as he awaited an opportunity to cross the Potomac River. Cox brought Booth and Henson food and liquor. It is inconceivable that Booth's condition would go from well and fleshy to gaunt and starved in just a few days.
5. It has been established with reasonable certainty that Booth broke his left leg as a result of his leap from the president's box onto the stage at Ford's Theater. It was the left leg that was treated by Dr. Mudd. According to Dr. John Franklin May, the corpse on the *Montauk* had a broken *right leg*.
6. It was stated the man killed at Garrett's wore brogans similar to those worn by Confederate soldiers. The left boot removed from the foot of John Wilkes Booth, which was in the possession of the War Department, was never compared to the footwear found on the corpse.
7. Regarding the body, it was never established with certainty which hand, arm, or wrist bore the initials "JWB."
8. Booth was known to carry large amounts of money. It has also been established that when he escaped he had approximately $6,500 in his possession. The man killed at Garrett's barn carried no cash. It is inconceivable Booth could have spent $6,500 during his escape—he had no opportunity.
9. Booth's keys were not found on the body. A set of keys found in the pockets of the coat belonging to the dead man did not fit anything that belonged to Booth.

10. Booth's personal watch, which he carried at all times, was not found on the body.
11. Booth's signet ring, one that he seldom failed to wear, was not found on the corpse.
12. The clothing worn by Booth during his escape, as described by Thomas A. Jones and others, was a suit of black broadcloth, the very same outfit he wore when he shot Lincoln. The man killed at Garrett's farm was wearing the uniform of a Confederate officer. James William Boyd was a Captain in the Confederate army.
13. It is clear from an analysis of subsequent testimony that no one among the party that captured and killed Booth was absolutely certain of his identity.
14. Conflicting, evasive, and confusing testimony by Dr. May and others regarding the body placed on the *Montauk* does nothing to firmly establish its identity as John Wilkes Booth. On close examination, May's testimony has the earmarks of one that was, at most, coerced and at least, qualified. In addition, it is quite apparent that his statement was modified by someone after it had been transcribed.
15. Not a single person who could authoritatively identify the remains of John Wilkes Booth was invited to the inquest aboard the *Montauk*.

If the man killed at Garrett's farm had truly been Booth, researchers would not be faced with this disturbing number of exceedingly contradictory elements. It causes the serious Booth scholar to wonder what actually took place on the morning of 26 April 1865. Clearly, the events of the time and place have generated confusing and contradictory testimony and reporting to the degree that one can safely conclude that no one actually knows what took place or who was killed.

The circumstances under which the man was shot and killed are likewise perplexing. No one knows for certain who fired the fatal shot, no one was certain of the identity of the body, and it seems strange that twenty-six troopers and three officers could not take a single crippled man alive if, indeed, that was their intention.

Why the contradicting and conflicting testimony? Why the veil of secrecy thrown over the matter by the federal government? Either the authorities were incredibly inept and sought to hide their mistakes, or the man that was killed was not John Wilkes Booth. Or both.

The confusion and contradiction regarding the man killed at the Garrett farm and placed aboard the *Montauk* are matched only by the confusion and contradiction relative to the disposal of the body.

Disposal of the Body

The traditionally accepted version of how the military disposed of the alleged body of John Wilkes Booth has it interred in the floor of a cell in the Old Arsenal Penitentiary. Such was the testimony of Col. Lafayette C. Baker, one that has been entered into the official record. Baker's testimony and those of others intended to support it, however, offer immediate contradictions. In some versions, the body is buried in a musket box, in others it is buried in a canvas shroud. To compound the confusion, other versions of the disposal have surfaced over the years.

In direct conflict with Baker's testimony, General Charles A. Dana stated that, to his certain knowledge, "the body was . . . buried under a slab in the navy yard and a battery of artillery hauled over it to obliterate any trace."

Detective William B. Wood provided another variation. He maintained the body was removed by Lafayette and Luther Baker from the *John S. Ide* after docking in Washington, placed in a small boat, and rowed to a small island twenty-seven miles downstream where it was buried. An unidentified man who claimed to have witnessed this burial corroborated Wood's version and added that the body was buried in quicklime.

Yet another version that differs markedly from the Baker testimony is given by a Captain E.W. Hilliard. Hilliard stated he was one of four men who removed the body from the Old Arsenal Penitentiary cell and transported it ten miles down the Potomac River where it was sunk. Hilliard also claimed the government manufactured the tale of Booth being buried just "to satisfy people."

Hilliard's version of what happened to the body is supported by a statement made by J.W. Edwards. During the time of the assassination, Edwards was a guard at the Washington jail. He stated the body of Booth had been "given into his custody at the jail, and that three men, claiming to be secret service agents, had taken the body away late at night, tied it to a plank with four cannon balls, and had sunk it in the Potomac River."

An article in the 21 June 1930 *Denver Republican* (reprinted from the *Washington Star*, date unknown), stated there were two bodies taken from the *Montauk*. One was delivered to the navy yard, the other was carried out to sea and dumped overboard.

In a startling revelation, retired Colonel James Hamilton Davidson, former commander of the 122nd Infantry, offers yet another version. At the time of the assassination, Davidson was in command of a post located at Portsmouth, Virginia. He claimed the head of the secret service, Col. Lafayette Baker, approached him on the evening of 27 April

1865 and requested a private meeting. Baker told Davidson he "brought into Portsmouth the body of Booth." Under orders from Baker, Davidson, along with six soldiers, carried the body to a warehouse basement, dug a grave, interred the body, and covered it with "sand . . . limestone, and dirt."

In addition to the several different versions of the disposal of the body, it must be pointed out that, in each case, *no one ever got a look at the corpse that was interred.*

In direct contrast with the practice of the day, the body of "Booth" was not placed on public display. Furthermore, completely disregarding another custom of the day, the body was not turned over to relatives, as occurred with Charles J. Guiteau, the assassin of President James Garfield, and with Leon Czolgolsz, the assassin of President William McKinley.

Another question: Why was the government, in truth, keeping the body from being seen or scrutinized? Why were they, in effect, hiding it? The only logical explanation must be that the body was not that of John Wilkes Booth.

Reburial

In response to a request from Edwin Booth, President Andrew Johnson ordered the body of "John Wilkes Booth" disinterred from the Old Arsenal Penitentiary and delivered to the Harvey and Marr Funeral Home in Washington, D.C.

If the body had been buried on an island, in Portsmouth, or dumped in the Potomac River or in the Atlantic Ocean as some claimed, then it could not have been dug up from the grounds of the Old Arsenal Penitentiary. In other words, the removal correlated with Baker's, the government's, version relative to the disposal of the body.

Rather than put an end to the web of contradictory and confusing elements associated with the mysterious body, the reburial simply added to the perplexing doubts.

The only truth regarding the reburial that can be determined is that a body was delivered by the government to the undertaker's shop in D.C. Following that, there occurred another series of conflicting testimonies and observations.

First of all, when the body arrived at the funeral home, it was wearing a black suit. Sometime between the killing in the barn and the delivery of the body, someone apparently removed the Confederate officer's uniform and replaced it with a black suit!

Secondly, according to the son of one of the undertakers, the body showed up wearing only one boot. Within a day, a second boot miraculously appeared!

The body was subsequently delivered to Weaver's in Baltimore. Here, it caused more identification problems.

Though the body was described by several as being only a skeleton, it was "positively" identified as John Wilkes Booth by a number of observers. Booth family friend Basil Moxley, however, confirmed what many were already thinking—the body was not that of Booth and family members knew it.

The prevailing evidence suggests that the body delivered to Baltimore was not the body of Booth, perhaps not even the same body that was identified on the *Montauk*. Were the bodies switched? If so, by whom? It may be that the government, at the request from Edwin Booth, was forced to provide a body, any body. There exists the distinct possibility that there may have actually been several bodies that were substituted at one time or another for that of John Wilkes Booth.

The Role of Edwin Booth

Some historians suspect Edwin Booth knew of his brother's escape all along, and played an important role in helping to keep it secret. During his later years, Basil Moxley stated that Edwin Booth knew all along his brother had escaped and that the body was merely a substitute.

On those rare occasions after April 1865 when Edwin spoke of his brother John Wilkes, it was always in the present tense, never the past. In addition, a man named Col. Young, who claimed he corresponded with Booth while the latter was living in India, said he was convinced Edwin knew John was alive and living in Bombay at the time.

When the alleged body of Booth lay in state at Sexton Weaver's quarters in Baltimore, Edwin never once looked at the remains to determine if it was, indeed, his own brother. Basil Moxley claimed Edwin had known all along the body was not that of his brother.

According to papers in the Neff collection, Henry Johnson, Booth's valet, returned to Maryland after serving his longtime employer, John Wilkes Booth, in England and India. Within days of his return, he went to work for Edwin Booth and, according to documents, remained with various members of the Booth family in Maryland and Massachusetts until he died.

The Return of John Wilkes Booth

Did John Wilkes Booth return to the United States and eventually die here? There exists no proof one way or the other, but information resulting from the research and writings of Izola Forrester, Finis Bates, and others strongly suggest he did.

Of the twenty or so men who have been identified as John Wilkes Booth over the years, most can be dismissed as a result of lack of evidence. Over the years, investigators keep returning to examine the possibility that John St. Helen/David E. George might have been the assassin. Unfortunately, too much time has passed and too many pertinent records missing or destroyed for a definitive conclusion to be reached.

Should the George mummy ever be located, a DNA test would determine identity. The George mummy, like John Wilkes Booth himself, remains elusive and mysterious.

Perhaps someday the mummy will be located. Maybe, with luck, a tenacious researcher will stumble onto an old trunk containing documents that can prove or disprove the contentions regarding the famous assassin of President Abraham Lincoln. Until then, we are forced to rely on available materials to derive conclusions about the people and events associated with the Lincoln assassination.

For many of us, patient, rational, and logical analysis of the evidence only leads to belief in the escape and return of the assassin John Wilkes Booth.

Appendix A

The Mystery of Boston Corbett

Boston Corbett has secured his place in history, right or wrong, as the man who shot and killed John Wilkes Booth.

At the time of the shooting, Corbett was a thirty-three-year-old first sergeant assigned to Company L of the Sixteenth New York Cavalry under the command of Lt. Doherty. He stood five feet five inches tall and possessed a rather unlikely background for a cavalryman.

Thomas H. Corbett was born in London, England, in 1832 and moved with his family to the United States when he was seven years old. The family moved often, and Corbett's childhood has often been characterized as troubled and unstable.

Corbett learned the hat-making trade as a youth while a resident of Troy, New York. Studies have shown that nitrate of mercury, the principle chemical used in treating felt in those days, can cause hallucinations, twitches, and psychoses. It is likely this chemical could have had a dramatic effect on Corbett. Corbett married when he was quite young. His wife and baby both died in childbirth, and Corbett subsequently took to drink, became an alcoholic, and lived on the streets of whatever town he traveled to. In Boston, Massachusetts, he was eventually taken in by a Methodist-run mission and baptized. Corbett, for reasons known only to him, changed his name to Boston during his christening.

Following his baptism, Corbett became a street preacher. He often spoke of hearing voices and seeing angels and other signs in the sky. Most researchers consider him mentally unstable.

Corbett presented an odd sight as he preached up and down New York City's Fulton Street. He allowed his hair to grow down to his waist because, as he told listeners, that was the way Christ wore His. During his street-preaching days in 1858, Corbett was approached by two prostitutes. The experience unnerved him to the degree that he castrated himself with a pair of scissors, an action he maintained was necessary for him to remain a holy man. He mangled his testicles so badly he was forced to spend a month recovering in Massachusetts General Hospital.

During the Civil War, Corbett joined the Union army, enlisting in Company I, Twelfth New York Militia. In the army, Corbett acquired a reputation as a religious zealot. He carried a Bible everywhere he went and read from it whenever the mood struck. Sometimes he even read it aloud in ranks, occasionally condemning his commanding officers for what he perceived to be violations of the Good Book's tenets.

Because of his bizarre behavior and tendency to refuse orders, Corbett was eventually court-martialed and sentenced to be shot. His sentence was later reduced and he was discharged from the army.

Somehow, Corbett was allowed to re-enlist in 1883. He was assigned to Company L, Sixteenth New York Cavalry and quickly rose to the rank of sergeant.

In June 1864, Corbett's troop was engaged in a fight with Rebel forces under the command of John Singleton Mosby. Corbett declined an option to surrender and instead opened fire on Mosby's raiders, fighting valiantly until he ran out of ammunition. He was subsequently captured and sent to Andersonville Prison and a few months later freed in a prisoner exchange.

Only minutes after the shooting of the man he believed was John Wilkes Booth, Corbett stated that "Providence directed me." At this, Corbett was derided by his fellow troopers. There were soldiers near Corbett during the incident, but no one actually saw him fire a shot, and his weapon was never examined. Lt. Ruggles stated, "No one saw Corbett fire, and one chamber of Booth's revolver held in his hand was empty, and I am by no means alone in the belief that he killed himself."

Corbett's claim was not corroborated by the testimony of a single witness. Many believed Corbett simply saw an opportunity to make the claim as the man who killed Booth and took it. The prevailing evidence does not support his contention.

When Corbett testified about the shooting at Garrett's barn, he claimed he accomplished the deed with a pistol. He told the court that, as he watched the fugitive closely and determined he was going to shoot his way out of the barn, he, Corbett, simply aimed and shot him. Richard B. Garrett said that was not true, that the man in the barn "made no movement to fire upon anybody." Ultimately, Corbett was legally credited with killing John Wilkes Booth.

The physicians who examined the body of the man presumed to be Booth all declared he had been shot by a pistol. Lt. Col. Everton J. Conger, an experienced officer who was on the scene at the barn, stated he heard only a pistol shot. The man identified as Booth carried a pistol in his hand; Corbett, according to all available research, carried only a rifle.

William Hanchett, in his book *The Lincoln Murder Conspiracies*, stated, "One thing is certain: the shot that killed [the man in the barn] had not been fired by the emotionally unbalanced trooper." Eisenschiml states that Corbett was, in fact, standing thirty feet away from the tobacco barn when the shot was fired, a position ordered by Conger. Some maintain that Corbett might have crawled up to a position adjacent the barn wall. If true, he would have been plainly seen by his fellow troopers, but none confirmed that this happened.

If Corbett actually shot and killed the man in the barn, then he was in direct violation of specific orders. Though he was charged with breach of military discipline, Corbett was never punished for disobedience. The original complaint was dismissed by Secretary of War Stanton, who many believe was anxious to put an end to the entire matter of John Wilkes Booth.

Corbett ultimately received a total of $1,653.85 reward for his participation in the capture and killing of Booth. For years afterward, he traveled the country as "The Man Who Killed Booth" and delivered lectures on his role in the killing.

In 1878 Corbett moved to Kansas where he homesteaded eighty acres near Concordia. Friends eventually secured him a position as a doorkeeper in January 1887 for the state House of Representatives. He had worked there only one month when, according to some accounts, he fired on and attempted to kill several members of the legislature. He was judged insane a short time later and confined in an asylum in Topeka.

Corbett escaped from the institution in May 1888. Accounts vary of Corbett's life afterward: Some believe he went to Mexico; others claimed he sold patent medicines from a wagon in Oklahoma; a few maintain he became a revivalist preacher in Texas. One oft-told account is that he appeared in Enid, Oklahoma, at the same time David E. George lived there. Some say he died there, but that has never been verified.

Ultimately, no one actually knows Corbett's role with regard to how the man in the burning barn met his death. The determination that Corbett was solely responsible for the killing was simply an easy and expeditious way to put an end to the case, and contemporary historians who have examined this incident maintain serious doubts that he fired the fatal shot.

Appendix B

The Question of Suicide

In spite of the governmental proposition that Boston Corbett shot and killed John Wilkes Booth, there is a consensus among contemporary researchers, wrote Theodore Roscoe in *The Web of Conspiracy*, that the man in Garrett's burning barn shot himself. The absolute truth will likely never be known, but serious doubt surrounds the contention that the trooper committed the deed, and evidence suggests the only reasonable explanation is that the fugitive died by his own hand.

The man in the barn, on being advised he was under arrest, stated he would never be taken alive. All of his actions, according to biographer Wilson, were those of a desperate man who meant to kill himself if capture were imminent.

W.J. Ferguson was told by one of the troopers present at Garrett's barn that the man shot himself. Lt. Col. Everton J. Conger was convinced that "Booth" shot himself. He stated that the victim "had the appearance of a man who put a pistol to his head and shot himself, shooting a little too low." Throughout his life, Conger never wavered from his contention. An experienced officer, Conger had seen many men die in battle and knew the nature of wounds.

As stated in Chapter X, the bullet entered the fugitive's neck on the right side and, following a downward course at an angle of approximately twenty degrees, penetrated three vertebrae, and passed out the left side. The probabilities of such a wound being inflicted from a distance are remote, according to researcher Otto Eisenschiml. If he was shot from some distance away, reasons Eisenschiml, he must have been "standing with his head bent sharply to the left and with his profile to the right wall and parallel to the door."

On the other hand, continues Eisenschiml, the wound incurred by the fugitive could have been self-inflicted "if he had held a pistol to the right side of his head and shot low." Since the fugitive was crippled and had thrown away his crutch, and since he was reacting under duress, Eisenschiml suggests this argument is a strong one.

Lieutenant Ruggles believed that the fugitive killed himself. "No one saw Corbett fire," he stated, "and one chamber of Booth's revolver... was empty."

Despite some logical and compelling arguments for suicide, some continue to maintain that the man in the barn was shot and killed not by Corbett, but by Everton Conger, who carried a pistol. At the time, Lt. Luther Baker was convinced Conger did the killing, and throughout the rest of his life he always held to that belief.

As commanding officers, either Baker, Conger, or Doherty could have ordered an examination of the firearms to determine which was used in the shooting. The truth is, not a single weapon—neither those carried by Corbett and Conger, nor the one in the possession of the fugitive or any others—was examined after the incident! Furthermore, according to David Miller Dewitt, had an autopsy been conducted on the body, it would have "disclosed the caliber of the pistol and the size of the ball with which the wound was inflicted." The War Department was in possession of the weapons carried by the dead man, and it would have been a simple task to examine them.

It must also be recalled that the examination of the body of the fugitive that was placed aboard the *Montauk* revealed what appeared to be a burn on the back of the neck. Such a burn, it has been suggested, could have resulted from the firing of a pistol at close range, as happens in a suicide.

Appendix C

The Lewis Paine/Lewis Thornton Powell Controversy

Lewis Paine, the tall, muscular, and enigmatic young man who was variously identified by a number of aliases and who figured heavily in the assassination conspiracy remains a mystery to this day.

Even his real name presents a problem to researchers. Author Chamlee states that "Lewis Payne" was actually not his name at all, that it was taken from a Lewis Paine of Fauquier, Virginia, who eventually went on to become a U.S. attorney for Wyoming Territory.

The government contended Lewis Paine (sometimes spelled Payne) and Lewis Thornton Powell were the same man, but there exists evidence that suggests otherwise. Researchers and authors Balsiger and Sellier claim they have discovered Civil War service records that provide a convincing case that Paine and Powell were two different men and that they were, in fact, cousins. Paine and Powell were apparently so similar in appearance that each was often confused with the other.

Balsiger and Sellier also state that they have obtained lost confession statements by conspiracy participants Michael O'Laughlin and George Atzerodt wherein they state that Paine and Powell were two separate individuals. They, O'Laughlin and Atzerodt, also suggested that Paine was arrested, tried, convicted, and executed for the attack on Secretary of State William Seward when, in fact, the crime was committed by Lewis Thornton Powell.

Researcher Vaughan Shelton has expressed belief in Paine's innocence relative to the attack on Seward and even goes so far as to claim the man known as Lewis Paine may not even have known Booth. Shelton's research, like that of Balsiger and Sellier, also supports the notion that Paine and Powell were two different men.

Based on documents he has located, Shelton believes Powell was an agent for Stanton's War Department and that he reported directly to Lafayette Baker. He also claims that Stanton's assistant Thomas Eckert made the contract with Powell to kill Seward. Major H.B. Smith, a Baltimore detective, was convinced Powell was a Union spy. After Paine was identified as Powell and subsequently hung for his alleged role in the conspiracy, says Shelton, the real Lewis Thornton Powell was therefore "legally" free to assume another identity.

Descriptions of Lewis Paine offered in the hundreds of publications about the conspiracy and assassination also add to the confusion. Writers have referred to Paine as "lacking mental capacity," having a "weak and sluggish intellect," "crazy," "demented," "mentally unbalanced," "insane," and "illiterate." Men such as this do not make good spies.

Conversely, a man sometimes identified as Powell is described as "almost sophisticated," "immaculately clad," "literate," and a man who played chess and euchre in the company of refined ladies.

These are, in fact, the descriptions of two different men.

Regarding the role of Paine in the conspiracy to assassinate Lincoln and Secretary of State William Seward, consider for a moment the strange events surrounding his capture. It will be recalled that Paine was taken into custody at the boardinghouse of Mary Surratt where he arrived late one evening while the occupants were being questioned by detectives. If Paine had actually attacked Seward not far away and only hours earlier, would he have been so stupid as to blunder into the Surratt house while Washington detectives were present? Such a thing is not likely.

Paine told the detectives he had been hired to dig a trench and came to find out what time he could begin working in the morning. Would a man who had been described as immaculately clad and almost sophisticated work at trench digging? Again, not likely. Author Eisenschiml wondered in print how Paine could just happen "to walk into Surratt's house while the prisoners were about to depart." Indeed. How?

Paine did not resist the arresting officers. In fact, he appeared not to have the slightest idea what was happening. Such is not the behavior of a guilty man.

Furthermore, Detective C.H. Rosch, who was among the officers who went to the Surratt house, observed that Paine did not behave as a man who had attacked the secretary of state, left him for dead, and surely knew he was being searched for by law enforcement authorities. According to Rosch, who was guarding the front of the Surratt house while the occupants were being questioned, he watched Paine approach the building. Rosch stated that the newcomer "peered at the porch numbers as he advanced." At approximately 11:20 P.M., says Rosch, he "saw [Paine] with a pickaxe over his shoulder go up the steps, knock, and ring at the door."

Searching for addresses would seem odd for a man who, according to the government, was well acquainted with the Surratt boardinghouse, had stayed there from time to time, and who was used to entering and leaving it at will. On the other hand, the behavior described by Rosch is consistent with one who had never been there before.

On seeing Paine, Mary Surratt proclaimed to the officers, "Before God, I do not know this man and have never seen him." Anna Surratt, Mary's daughter, who had spent some time with Lewis Powell, denied ever seeing Paine before.

William Seward's servant, William Bell, identified Paine as the secretary of state's assailant from a lineup at Augur's headquarters. William E. Doster, defense attorney for Paine and Atzerodt, maintained in court that the lineup was rigged.

If, indeed, Paine and Powell were two different men who were look-alikes, that may, in part, explain many of the discrepancies in the historical record. According to researchers, Paine's movements were hard to follow during the unfolding of the conspiracy. If Paine were constantly being confused with Powell, then it is easy to see why such a thing could happen.

In yet another mysterious development, Lewis Paine, following his arrest, was placed in the personal custody of Major Thomas T. Eckert, normally a job for an ordinary detective. Eckert kept Paine in isolation for days, allowing no one near him but himself. Why an assistant secretary of war was assigned to such an ordinary task remains unexplained.

Could Lewis Paine have been set up? If so, it was in the best interests of those involved to keep him isolated and incommunicado.

Following Paine's execution, his body went unclaimed. Had it been the body of Lewis Thornton Powell, it is likely it would have been claimed by one of several family members.

Researchers and scholars, unaware that Paine and Powell were two different men, could have bungled in their interpretations and mixed their respective identities and activities. Such mistakes are not unknown in historical research.

Appendix D

The Mystery of John Parker

A curious and still unresolved mystery surrounds John Parker, the White House guard assigned to protect President Lincoln on the night of the assassination but who, instead, abandoned his post.

According to documents, Parker, born in 1830 in Virginia, had little or no education, used coarse language, and was of questionable character. Author Roscoe represents him as "desolate, craven . . . a drunken good-for-nothing who had one of the worst records on the whole Washington force."

Parker joined the Washington Metropolitan Police force in 1861. Throughout his tenure as a D.C. policeman, he had a rather unimpressive, even puzzling record. Not long after beginning his employment, he was charged with conduct unbecoming an officer and using "violent, coarse, and insolent language." During a subsequent hearing, Parker was described as showing a "disposition to be insubordinate." Parker was returned to duty with no punishment.

In March 1863 Parker was charged with "willful violation of rules and regulations and conduct unbecoming an officer." It seems Parker verbally abused a fellow officer, visited a house of prostitution, became drunk, and fired a pistol through a window. The charges were subsequently dismissed.

Three weeks later, Parker was discovered sleeping while on duty. The charges were dismissed. In June 1863 Parker was charged with insulting a woman. Once again, charges were dismissed.

On 3 August of the same year, Parker was charged with "general inefficiency"—he had been absent forty-one out of eighty-two working days! Charges were dismissed.

On 2 April 1864 Parker was charged with insubordination, using disrespectful language, and gross neglect of duty. He was tried and a judgement made that he be dismissed from the force. He was, but subsequently reinstated seven months later.

With such a record, one wonders why Parker remained on the force. Researchers have suggested that someone was looking out for Parker, protecting him, and perhaps planning on using him for some special assignment in the future.

During the first week of April 1865, Washington Metro Police received a request that Parker be assigned to duty at the White House as a guard. Of all of the officers on the force, Parker seemed like the most unlikely candidate to be selected for such an important job. Subsequent investigation has revealed that Parker was specifically requested by Mary Todd Lincoln, the wife of the president! Though it was not within her authority to do so, Mrs. Lincoln fired one of the special guards and filled the vacancy with Parker. Even Abraham Lincoln himself openly doubted Parker's reliability.

The appointment of Parker as a special guard by the first lady has mystified scholars for well over a century. Author

Theodore Roscoe, however, offers a perspective that carries with it some troubling logic—he suggests Mary Todd Lincoln may have been "involved" with John Parker. It would not have been the first time Mrs. Lincoln had misbehaved. She was, according to Roscoe, guilty of several indiscretions, one with a White House gardener.

On the night of the assassination, Parker, dressed in civilian clothes and armed with a .38 revolver, had specific orders to remain stationed outside the door to the president's theater box and allow no one to enter. In short, he was given the responsibility of protecting the president.

After remaining seated outside the door for a portion of the play, Parker left to get a drink at a nearby saloon, leaving the box completely unguarded. Was this mere carelessness or lack of responsibility on his part, or was it planned?

Prior to Parker's departure from his station, a Captain Theodore McGowan, who was watching the play, claimed he saw John Wilkes Booth pass by his aisle, approach the guard, and hand him a note or a card. Minutes later, Parker was gone, his post deserted.

When the activity associated with the assassination and the pursuit, capture, and killing of "Booth" died down, police superintendent A.C. Richards filed charges against Parker for dereliction of duty. He was tried on 3 May and, in a surprising move, the complaint was dismissed on 2 June. Parker was never reprimanded, and soon afterward was *returned to duty as a White House guard*! Records of the trial and who testified were removed from files and have not been seen since. Some are even convinced Mary Todd Lincoln had a hand in the dismissal of the charges against Parker.

Why was Parker released? A number of historians are convinced Parker was part of a conspiracy headed by

Secretary of War Stanton. It was Stanton's responsibility to see that the president was protected. On the afternoon prior to the assassination, Lincoln requested specific bodyguards, including Thomas Eckert. In a curious act, he was refused by Stanton. Researchers agree that if Eckert had accompanied Lincoln to Ford's Theater that night, the assassination would never have happened. Instead, a completely irresponsible and unreliable guard was sent. Was Eckert aware of a plot to kill the president that evening? Was Stanton? It would seem so.

During the war, Stanton mercilessly court-martialed sentries who had fallen asleep at their posts. It seems odd that he forgave Parker for leaving his post and allowing the president of the United States to be killed. Was Stanton protecting Parker? If so, for what reason? The evidence suggests a governmental cover-up.

Shortly after Secretary of War Stanton was removed from office in 1868, John Parker was dismissed from the police force for allegedly sleeping in a streetcar while on duty. Having survived so many far more serious offenses, it is odd that this particular transgression got him fired. Shortly after Parker left the force, he disappeared, and to this day no one knows his fate.

Appendix E

The Mystery of the Diary

One of the greatest mysteries surrounding the Lincoln assassination is related to the so-called diary allegedly found on the body of the man killed at Garrett's farm. Some writers refer to it as a "personal diary," others call it a "memorandum book," still others have referred to it as a "notebook." It has often been described as being bound by "red Moroccan leather."

Author Chamlee writes that it was "an outdated 1864 diary [used] mostly as scratch paper... [serving] as a combination wallet and notebook."

According to most historical accounts, the diary was found among the possessions of the fugitive. It was apparently handed around to some of the soldiers present, for some accounts mention that several of them made copies of the contents. Ultimately, the diary was gathered up by Conger, along with the rest of the victim's belongings, and transported to Washington.

On arriving in the capital, Conger turned over all the items, including the diary, to Lafayette Baker who in turn delivered it to Secretary of War Stanton. Stanton examined each one of the items and returned them to Baker, all except the diary. The secretary kept the diary overnight and on the following day gave it to Thomas Eckert, who locked it in a War Department safe. It was not seen again for two years. When the diary was finally removed from the safe, eighteen pages were missing!

A major mystery associated with the diary is related to the fact that it was not introduced as evidence during the Conspiracy Trial in 1865. All other items taken from the body on the morning of 26 April 1865 such as the knife, pistols, and compass were introduced as evidence. The one item taken from the body not provided was the diary, considered by historians as perhaps the single most vital piece of evidence associated with the conspiracy.

Francis Wilson writes that many were aware of the existence of the diary at the time of the Conspiracy Trial. Critics of the government claim Stanton, and perhaps others, suppressed the diary as evidence because it contained information critical of governmental leaders. The missing pages, it is believed, were torn out by someone in order to remove evidence of such.

On one of the pages that remained in the diary, Booth wrote that he intended to return to Washington to "clear my name." What could he possibly have meant by this and how did he intend to clear his name? In the diary, Booth used words such as "we" and "our," indicating he was not alone in his efforts. Did clearing his name have anything to do with the missing pages? Did the diary contain incriminating evidence? It would seem so. Otherwise, why was it kept secret for two years?

Congressman Benjamin Butler speculated that Booth's diary "could have proved who it was that changed Booth's purpose from capture to assassination." Butler also suggested that the person who would benefit most from Lincoln's death was Andrew Johnson.

A second mystery revolves around the copies of the diary made by soldiers on 26 April 1865. That copies were made was, in fact, verified by Lafayette Baker. Why, one wonders, would troopers have gone to the trouble to make copies unless the book contained some relevant, perhaps provocative information? Once Stanton learned copies had been made, he immediately ordered all of them turned over to him at once. This is curious, since an examination of the extant pages reveals nothing of major significance.

Lt. Col. Conger also admitted making a copy of the diary while it was in his possession and before he turned it over to Baker. What became of Conger's copy is not known.

A third mystery concerns the eighteen missing pages. During questioning in 1867, Lafayette Baker stated with confidence that the dairy he examined in 1867 was not in the same condition as the one he delivered to Stanton in 1865. Since that time, he said, it had been "mutilated."

When the diary was found, according to Baker, there were no pages missing. Baker recalled there was a great deal more to the notebook when he first saw it, and he remembered reading portions of the diary that contained passages not present in the one produced in 1867. Baker also related that he remembered seeing a drawing of a house in the diary he first examined, a drawing not found in the 1867 version. He further stated that cards and pieces of paper with names were also missing from the back cover pocket.

Lt. Col. Everton Conger, after examining the diary in 1867, stated he thought it "read a little differently" when he examined it two years earlier.

Stanton, on the other hand, claimed that the eighteen pages were missing from the diary when it was given to him. If the diary did possess evidence potentially incriminating to him, that is what he would be expected to say.

Experts who have examined the diary closely, according to writer George S. Bryan, declare it is evident that a heavy knife lopped away the missing pages in one batch. Is it likely Booth would have done such a thing? Or is it more likely, as some have suggested, that Stanton, on reading incriminating evidence, removed all the pages at once. The remaining edges of the cut out pages show they had been written on.

The findings of Balsiger and Sellier offer another mystery. They contend Booth's diary was found at a temporary campsite near Gambo Creek on 22 April and delivered to Stanton soon afterward by NDP detectives Bernard and Dooley. Stanton, according to the papers of George Julian, showed the diary to him, John Conness, Thomas Eckert, and Zachariah Chandler. All agreed the diary contained incriminating evidence.

If true, how does one account for the diary found on the body of the man at Garrett's farm. One possibility is that James William Boyd himself carried a similar diary. The other possibility, and one that has been suggested over the years, is that the "Booth" diary was actually a forgery masterminded by governmental officials and was planted on Boyd. The notion that the Booth diary was a forgery has been bandied about by historians for over a century.

The diary found on the body allegedly contained several photographs of women known to consort with Booth. While many apparently examined the diary at Garrett's farm, there was never any mention of the photographs until the diary was in the hands of Stanton in Washington D.C. The missing pages of Booth's diary, say Balsiger and Sellier, were found among the papers of Stanton's descendants.

Whatever the truth, the fact remains that the diary, one of the most valuable pieces of evidence in the entire Lincoln assassination episode, was kept hidden for two years and clearly tampered with before it was finally brought forth.

Bibliography

Books

Abbott, Abbott A. *The Assassination and Death of Abraham Lincoln, President of the United States of America*. New York: American News Co. 1865.

Arnold, Samuel Bland. *Defense and Prison Experiences of a Lincoln Conspirator, Statements and Autographed Notes*. Hattiesburg, Mississippi: Book Farm. 1943.

Baker, Lafayette C. *History of the United States Secret Service*. Philadelphia: King and Baird. 1868.

Balsiger, David, and Sellier, Charles E. *The Lincoln Conspiracy*. Los Angeles: Schick Sunn Classic Books. 1977.

Basler, Roy P. *The Lincoln Legend*. Boston: Houghton Mifflin Company. 1935.

Bates, David Homer. *Lincoln in the Telegraph Office*. New York: D. Appleton-Century Company. 1907.

______. *Some Recollections of Abraham Lincoln*. New York: The Grafton Press. 1906.

Bates, Finis L. *Escape and Suicide of John Wilkes Booth, Assassin of President Lincoln*. Memphis: Pilcher Printing Co. 1907.

Beyer, William Gilmore. *On Hazardous Service*. New York: Harper and Brothers. 1912.

Bishop, James A. *The Day Lincoln Was Shot*. New York: Harper and Brothers. 1955.

Borrenson, Ralph. *When Lincoln Died*. New York: Appleton-Century. 1965.

Bryan, George S. *The Great American Myth*. New York: Carrick and Evans. 1940.

Buckingham, J.E. *Reminiscences and Souvenirs of the Assassination of Abraham Lincoln*. Washington: Press of Rufus H. Darby. 1894.

Burnett, Henry L. *Assassination of President Lincoln and the Trial of the Assassins*. New York: Ohio Society of New York. 1906.

______. *Some Incidents in the Trial of President Lincoln's Assassins*. New York: D. Appleton. 1891.

Campbell, Helen Jones. *The Case For Mrs. Surratt*. New York: G.P. Putnam's Sons, 1943.

Campbell, W. P. *The Escape and Wanderings of John Wilkes Booth Until Final Ending of the Trial by Suicide in Enid, Oklahoma, January 12, 1903*. Oklahoma City: Self-published. 1922.

Carter, Samuel. *The Riddle of Dr. Mudd*. New York: G.P. Putnam's Sons. 1974.

Chamlee, Roy Z. *Lincoln's Assassins: A Complete Account of Their Capture, Trial, and Punishment*. Jefferson, North Carolina: McFarland and Company, Inc. 1924.

Clarke, Asia Booth. *A Memoir of John Wilkes Booth by His Sister, The Unlocked Book*. (Ed. Eleanor Farjeon). London: Faber and Faber, Ltd. 1938.

______. *The Elder and the Younger Booth*. Boston: James R. Osgood. 1882.

Cottrell, John. *Anatomy of an Assassination*. New York: Funk and Wagnalls. 1966.

Crozier, R.H. *The Bloody Junto; or, The Escape of John Wilkes Booth*. Little Rock, Arkansas: Woodruff and Blocher. 1869.

Cuthbert, Norma B. (Ed.). *Lincoln and the Baltimore Plot*. San Marino, California: The Huntington Library. 1949.

DeWitt, David Miller. *The Assassination of Abraham Lincoln and Its Expiation*. New York: Macmillan. 1909.

Dye, John Smith. *A History of the Plots and Crimes of the Great Conspiracy*. New York: Self-published. 1866.

Eisenschiml, Otto. *In the Shadow of Lincoln's Death*. New York: Wilfred Funk, Inc. 1950.

_______. *Why Was Lincoln Murdered?* Boston: Little, Brown, and Co. 1937.

Ferguson, William F. *I Saw Booth Shoot Lincoln*. Cambridge: Houghton Mifflin, The Riverside Press. 1930.

Flower, Frank A. *Edwin McMasters Stanton*. Akron, Ohio: The Sadfield Publishing Co. 1905.

Forrester, Izola. *This One Mad Act*. Boston: Hale, Cushman, and Flynt. 1937.

Fowler, Robert H. *Album of the Lincoln Murder*. Harrisburg, Pennsylvania: Stackpole Books. 1965.

Good, Timothy S. *We Saw Lincoln Shot: One Hundred Eyewitness Accounts*. Jackson: University Press of Mississippi. 1995.

Gorham, George C. *Life and Public Services of Edwin M. Stanton*, 2 vols. Boston: Houghton, Mifflin and Co. 1899.

Grant, Ulysses S. *Personal Memoirs of U.S. Grant*, Vols I, II, and III. New York: Charles L. Webster and Company. 1886.

Gutman, Richard J.S., and Gutman, Kellie O. *John Wilkes Booth Himself*. Dover, Massachusetts: Hired Hand Press. 1979.

Hall, James O. *Note on the John Wilkes Booth Escape Route*. Clinton, Maryland: The Surratt Society. 1980.

Hanchett, William. *The Lincoln Murder Mysteries*. Chicago: University of Illinois Press. 1983.

Harris, Thomas Mealey. *The Assassination of Lincoln, A History of the Great Conspiracy: Trial of the Conspirators by a Military*

Commission and a Review of the Trial of John H. Surratt. Boston: American Citizens Co. 1897.

Higdon, Hal. *The Union vs. Dr. Mudd.* Chicago: Follett Publishing Co. 1964.

Johnson, Byron Berkeley. *Abraham Lincoln and Boston Corbett.* Waltham, Boston: Lincoln and Smith Press 1914.

Johnson, Robert Underwood, and Buel, Clarence Clough. *Battles and Leaders of the Civil War, Vol. IV.* New York: The Century Co. 1888.

Jones, Evan R. *Lincoln and Stanton, Historical Sketches.* London: Frederick Warne and Co. 1875.

Jones, Thomas A. *J. Wilkes Booth. An Account of His Sojourn in Southern Maryland . . . and His Death in Virginia.* Chicago: Laird and Lee. 1893.

Kimmel, Stanley. *The Mad Booths of Maryland, 2nd Ed.* New York: Dover Publications. 1969.

Kunhardt, Dorothy Meserve, and Kunhardt, Philip B. Jr. *Twenty Days.* New York: Castle Books. 1965.

Lamon, Ward H. *Recollections of Abraham Lincoln.* Chicago: A.C. McClurg and Company. 1895.

Laughlin, Clara E. *The Death of Lincoln: The Story of Booth's Plot, His Deed and the Penalty.* New York: Doubleday and Co. 1909.

Lewis, Lloyd. *Myths After Lincoln.* New York: Harcourt, Brace and Co. 1929.

Logan, John A. *The Great Conspiracy.* New York: A.R. Hart and Company. 1886.

McCarty, Burke. *The Suppressed Truth About the Assassination of Abraham Lincoln.* Philadelphia: Burke McCarty, Publisher. 1924.

McLaughlin, Emmett. *An Inquiry into the Assassination of Abraham Lincoln.* New York: Lyle Stuart, Inc. 1963.

Mearns, David C. *The Lincoln Papers*. Garden City, New York: Doubleday. 1948.

Morse, John T. Jr. *Abraham Lincoln*. Boston: Houghton Mifflin Company. 1921.

Mudd, Samuel A. (Mudd, Nettie, Ed.). *The Life of Dr. Samuel A. Mudd*. New York: The Neale Publishing Co. 1906.

Oldroyd, Osborn H. *The Assassination of Abraham Lincoln, Flight, Pursuit, Capture, and Punishment of the Conspirators*. Washington, D.C.: Self-published. 1914.

Pinkerton, Allan. *Spy of the Rebellion*. New York: G.W. Carleton and Company. 1883.

Pitman, Benn (Compiler). *The Assassination of President Lincoln and the Trial of the Conspirators*. New York: Funk and Wagnalls. 1954.

Poore, Benjamin Perley. *The Conspiracy Trial for the Murder of the President: And the Attempt to Overthrow the Government by the Assassination of its Principal Officers*. Boston: J.E. Tilton and Co. 1865.

Pratt, Fletcher. *Stanton, Lincoln's Secretary of War.* Westport, Connecticut: Rumford Press. 1949.

Roscoe, Theodore. *The Web of Conspiracy: The Complete Story of the Men Who Murdered Abraham Lincoln*. Englewood Cliffs, New Jersey: Prentice Hall. 1959.

Samples, Gordon. *Lust For Fame: The Stage Career of John Wilkes Booth*. Jefferson, North Carolina: McFarland and Company, Inc., Publishers. 1982.

Shelton, Vaughan. *Mask For Treason: The Lincoln Murder Trial*. Harrisburg, Pennsylvania: Stackpole Books. 1965.

Skinner, Otis. *The Mad Folk of the Theater.* New York: Bobbs-Merrill Company. 1928.

Smoot, R.M. *The Unwritten History of the Assassination of Abraham Lincoln*. Baltimore: John Murphy Company. 1904.

Starkey, Larry. *Wilkes Booth Came to Washington*. New York: Random House. 1976.

Starr, John W. Jr. *Lincoln's Last Day*. New York: Stokes. 1922.

Stern, Philip Van Doren. *The Man Who Killed Lincoln*. New York: Random House. 1939.

Tanner, James. *While Lincoln Lay Dying*. Philadelphia: Union League of Philadelphia. 1868.

Tarbell, Ida M. *The Life of Abraham Lincoln*. New York: The Macmillan Company. 1928.

Townsend, George Alfred. *The Life, Crime, and Capture of John Wilkes Booth*. New York: Dick and Fitzgerald Publishers. 1865.

Walker, Dale L. *Legends and Lies: Great Mysteries of the American West*. New York: A Tom Doherty Associates Book. 1997.

Weichmann, Louis J. *A True History of the Assassination of Abraham Lincoln and the Conspiracy of 1865*, Ed. F.E. Risvold. New York: Alfred A. Knopf. 1975.

Wilson, John Francis. *John Wilkes Booth: Fact and Fiction of Lincoln's Assassination*. Boston: Houghton Mifflin. 1929.

Articles

Arnold, Samuel Bland, "Lincoln Conspiracy and Conspirators," *Ohio State Journal*. 10-20 December 1902.

Baker, L.B. "An Eyewitness Account of the Death and Burial of J. Wilkes Booth," *Journal of the Illinois State Historical Society*, No. 39. December 1946.

Crook, William H. "Lincoln's Last Day," *Harper's Monthly*. September 1907.

Davis, William C. "The Lincoln Conspiracy—Hoax?" *Civil War Times Illustrated*. November 1977.

DeMotte, William H. "The Assassination of Abraham Lincoln," *Journal of the Illinois State Historical Society*, No. 20. October 1927.

Doherty, Edward P. "Pursuit and Death of John Wilkes Booth: Captain Doherty's Narrative," *Century Magazine*. January 1890.

Ford, John T. "Behind the Curtain of a Conspiracy," *North American Review*. September 1888.

Fowler, Robert H. "New Evidence in the Lincoln Murder Conspiracy," *Civil War Times illustrated*. February 1965.

______. "Was Stanton Behind Lincoln's Murder?" *Civil War Times*. August 1961.

Fulton, Justin D. "Behind the Purple Curtain: Lincoln's Assassins," *Christian Heritage*. April/May 1979.

Garrett, Richard Baynham. "A Chapter of Unwritten History... Account of the Flight and Death of John Wilkes Booth." *Virginia Magazine of History and Biography*, No. 71. October 1963.

Garrett, William H. "True Story of the Capture of John Wilkes Booth," *Confederate Veteran Magazine*. April 1921. p. 130.

Giddens, Paul H. "Ben Pitman on the Trial of Lincoln's Assassins," *Tyler's Quarterly Historical and Genealogical Magazine*. July 1940. p. 12. pp. 485-493.

Gleason, D.H.L. "Conspiracy Against Lincoln," *The Magazine of History*. February 1911. pp. 59-65.

Hall, James O. "The Mystery of Lincoln's Guard," *Surratt Society News*. May 1982.

Hanchett, William. "Booth's Diary," *Journal of the Illinois State Historical Society*, No. 72. February 1979.

Head, Constance. "John Wilkes Booth as a Hero Figure," *Journal of American Culture*, No. 5. Fall 1982.

_______. "Insights on John Wilkes Booth from His Sister Asia's Correspondence," *Lincoln Herald*, No. 82. Winter 1980.

King, Horatio. "The Assassination of President Lincoln," *New England Magazine*. December 1893. pp. 430-431.

Laughlin, Clara. "The Last Twenty-four Hours of Lincoln's Life," *Ladies' Home Journal*. February 1909.

May, John F. "The Mark of the Scalpel," *Records of the Columbia Historical Society*. Vol. VIII. 1910.

McBride, Robert W. "Lincoln's Body Guard," *Indiana Historical Society Publications*. Vol. V. 1911.

Moss, M. Helen Palmes. "Lincoln and Wilkes Booth as Seen on the Day of the Assassination," *Century Magazine*. April 1909.

Munroe, Seaton, "Recollections of Lincoln's Assassination," *North American Review*. April 1896.

Morris, Clara. "Some Reflections of John Wilkes Booth," *McClure's Magazine*. February 1901.

Peck, Harry Thurston. "Dewitt's 'Assassination of Abraham Lincoln,'" *Bookman*. April 1909.

Porter, George Loring. "How Booth's Body Was Hidden," *Magazine of History*, No. 38. 1929.

Rankin, Mrs. McKee. "The News of Lincoln's Death," *American Magazine*. January 1909.

Reid, Albert T. "Boston Corbett: The Man of Mystery of the Lincoln Drama," *Scribner's Magazine*. July 1929.

Ruggles, M.B. "Pursuit and Death of John Wilkes Booth: Major Ruggles's Narrative," *Century Magazine*, No. 39. January 1890.

Shepherd, William G. "Shattering the Myth of John Wilkes Booth's Escape," *Harper's Magazine*, November 1924.

Skinner, Otil. "The Last of John Wilkes Booth," *American Magazine*. November 1908.

Speed, James. "The Assassins of Lincoln," *North American Review*. September 1888.

Stimmel, Smith. "Experiences as a Member of President Lincoln's Body Guard," *North Dakota Historical Quarterly*. January 1927.

Surratt, John H. "Lecture on the Lincoln Conspiracy," *Lincoln Herald*, No. 51. December 1949.

Taylor, W.H. "A New Story of the Assassination of Lincoln," *Leslie's Weekly*, 26 March 1908.

Tilton, Clint C. "First Plot Against Lincoln," *National Republic*. February 1936.

Tindal, William. "Booth's Escape From Washington," *Records of the Columbia Historical Society*. Vol. XVIII, 1915.

Townsend, George Alfred. "How Wilkes Booth Crossed the Potomac," *Century Magazine*. April 1884. pp. 822-832.

Weik, Jesse W. "A New Story of Lincoln's Assassination," *Century Magazine*. February 1913.

Newspapers

Arnold, Samuel B. "The Lincoln Plot," *Baltimore American*. 8-20 December 1902.

Baltimore American. 6 June 1903.

______. 16 February 1869.

Black, F.L. "David E. George as John Wilkes Booth," *Dearborn Independent*. 25 April 1925.

______. "Identification of J. Wilkes Booth," *Dearborn Independent.* 2 May 1925.

Boston *Sunday Globe*. 12 December 1897.

Hathaway, Carson C. "What the Mark of the Scalpel Tells," *Dearborn Independent*. 7 Feb 1925.

McNutt, Michael. "Sleuths Seek Mummified Mystery Body," *Saturday Oklahoman and Times*. 22 June 1991.

New York *Tribune*. 15 April 1865.

New York World. 15 April 1892.

Sciolino, Elaine. "Assassins Usually Miss the Larger Target," *The New York Times*. 12 November 1995.

Washington *Daily Morning Chronicle*. 15 April 1865.

Documents

Office of the Provost Marshal, National Archives.

Records of the District of Columbia, Police Blotter, Detective Corps, 14-19 April 1865. National Archives.

Records of the Judge Advocate General, Investigation and Trial Papers—Assassination of President Lincoln. Microfilm 599. National Archives.

Index

Other books from Republic of

Best Tales of Texas Ghosts

Docia Schultz Williams

A spirited medley of spine-tingling tales and a collection of the most haunting stories from the Texas Ghost Series.

400 pages • 1-55622-569-5 • $17.95

The Return of the Outlaw Billy the Kid

W.C. Jameson & Frederic Bean

Takes careful aim at the controversial evidence and allows the readers to judge for themselves: Who was Billy the Kid?

272 pages • 1-55622-584-9 • $16.95

Texas Ranger Tales
Stories That Need Telling

Mike Cox

A collection of legendary Ranger stories, arranged chronologically, from new takes on the famous tales to fresh stories few, if any, will have heard.

336 pages • 1-55622-537-7 • $16.95

The Last of the Old-Time Cowboys

Patrick Dearen

From those who lived it, the author collected priceless, spellbinding stories of a simpler era when a man's word was his bond and a cowhand rode hard and lived harder.

260 pages • 1-55622-613-6 • $16.95

The Texas Golf Guide

Art Stricklin

A comprehensive reference to golf courses in the state of Texas, combining basic information about each course including name, address, phone number, and prices.

304 pages • 1-55622-575-X • $14.95

First in the Lone Star State: A Texas Brag Book

Sherrie S. McLeRoy

Unique people, places, events, inventions, and products for Texas trivia buffs.

256 pages • 1-55622-572-5 • $14.95

Texas Press and Seaside Press

Bubba Speak
Texas Folk Sayings

W.C. Jameson

A thesaurus of language unique to Texas culture, *Bubba Speak* is almost required reading for anyone new to the state of Texas.

186 pages • 1-55622-616-0 • $14.95

Texas Wit and Wisdom

Wallace O. Chariton

Filled with friendly, entertaining stories, anecdotes, amusing quotations, funny signs, classic Texas jokes, and surprisingly sound advice from the often wacky but always wonderful world of Texans.

256 pages • 1-55622-257-2 • $12.95

Fixin' to Be Texan

Helen Bryant

This book is an essential tool to understanding the wonderful (and sometimes incomprehensible) behavior of the native population of the state.

240 pages • 1-55622-648-9 • $15.95

Lawmen of the Old West: The Good Guys

Del Cain

Twelve good men seeking an honorable life and justice in the early West.

240 pages • 1-55622-677-2 • $16.95

Unsolved Texas Mysteries

Chariton, Young, and Eckhardt

The authors present the known facts and circumstances of unsolved mysteries such as the lost documents of the Alamo, the Army's buried gun cache, and Booth's alleged escape and life in Central Texas.

272 pages • 1-55622-256-4 • $16.95

Unsolved Mysteries of the Old West

W.C. Jameson

New insights and revealing information on questions such as: Who is really buried in Jesse James' grave? Who killed Belle Starr? and Who has Pancho Villa's head?

256 pages • 1-55622-641-1 • $16.95

Other books from Republic of Texas Press and Seaside Press

Alamo Movies
Alamo Story: From Early History to Current Conflicts
At Least 1836 Things You Ought to Know About Texas But Probably Don't

Battlefields of Texas
Best Tales of Texas Ghosts
Bubba Speak: Texas Folk Sayings
A Cowboy of the Pecos
Critter Chronicles
Dallas Uncovered (2nd Edition)
Daughter of Fortune: The Bettie Brown Story
Defense of a Legend
Dirty Dining
Etta Place: Her Life and Times with Butch Cassidy and the Sundance Kid
Exotic Pets: A Veterinary Guide for Owners
Exploring Branson: A Family Guide
Exploring Dallas with Children (2nd Edition)
Exploring New Orleans: A Family Guide
Exploring San Antonio with Children
Exploring Texas with Children
Exploring the Alamo Legends

Eyewitness to the Alamo
First in the Lone Star State
Fixin' to Be Texan
The Funny Side of Texas
Ghosts Along the Texas Coast
Ghosts of the Alamo
Good Times in Texas
The Great Texas Airship Mystery
Horses and Horse Sense
King Ranch Story
The Last of the Old-Time Cowboys
Lawmen of the Old West
Letters Home: A Soldier's Legacy
Making it Easy: Cajun Cooking

New Orleans Greys
Phantoms of the Plains
Puncher Pie
Rainy Days in Texas Funbook
Red River Women
Return of Assassin John Wilkes Booth
Return of the Outlaw Billy the Kid
Return of the Outlaw Butch Cassidy
Spindletop Unwound
Spirits of San Antonio and South Texas
Tales of the Guadalupe Mountains
The Texas Golf Guide
Texas Highway Humor
Texas Ranger Tales
Texas Ranger Tales II
Texas Tales Your Teacher Never Told You
Texas Wit and Wisdom
That Cat Won't Flush
They Don't Have to Die
This Dog'll Hunt
Top Texas Chefs Cook at Home: Favorite Entrees
Trail Rider's Guide to Texas

Treasury of Texas Trivia
Unsolved Mysteries of the Old West
Unsolved Texas Mysteries
Ultimate Chili Cookbook
When Darkness Falls
Wild Camp Tales
Your Kitten's First Year
Your Puppy's First Year